Sabine Dardenne chose to write this book for three reasons: 'so that people stop giving me strange looks and treating me like a curiosity; so that no one asks me any more questions ever again; and so that the judicial system never again frees a paedophile for "good behaviour"'. She testified at the trial of Marc Dutroux in 2004, eight years after her kidnapping. He was condemned to prison for life.

Praise for *I Choose to Live*:

'Remarkable' *Sunday Telegraph*

'*I Choose to Live* is Sabine's dignified, restrained and ultimately uplifting testimony' *Big Issue*

'Sabine's testimony enters the highest rank of tales of epic survival' *Glasgow Herald*

'Sabine's book is a welcome break from the "victim culture" and, as she says, offers ample reasons why paedophiles should not be let out for "good behaviour"' *TES*

'Sabine humbled witnesses to Dutroux's trial last year when she calmly delivered the evidence that sentenced her tormentor to life imprisonment. This book is testament to her courage' *Sunday Express*

I Choose to Live

SABINE DARDENNE

with MARIE-THÉRÈSE CUNY

Translated by PENELOPE DENING

Virago

VIRAGO

First published in Great Britain in April 2005 by Virago Press
This paperback edition published in January 2006 by Virago Press
Reprinted 2006 (six times)
Published in France by Oh! Editions, Paris, in 2004
as *J'avais 12 ans, j'ai pris mon vélo et je suis partie à l'école . . .*

A CIP catalogue record for this book
is available from the British Library

ISBN-13: 978-1-84408-268-1
ISBN-10: 1-84408-268-7

Typeset in Goudy by M Rules
Printed and bound in Great Britain by
Clays Ltd, St Ives plc

Virago Press
An imprint of
Time Warner Book Group UK
Brettenham House
Lancaster Place
London WC2E 7EN

www.virago.co.uk

To all the victims

CONTENTS

I was 12 years old and I took my bike

My name is Sabine. I used to live in a little village in Belgium, until one day, on my way to school, I disappeared. I was twelve years old. At first the police thought that I'd run away, and for a long time my parents prayed that they were right. At night my mother would leave a light on in the house, and open one of the shutters. Just in case . . . My grandmother would leave her front door unlocked with the same idea.

I had always been a bit of a rebel, very independently minded, and never one to let myself be trampled on without a fight. I was forever rowing with my older sisters and with my mother. On that particular morning I had taken with me my school report slips, each subject duly signed by my mother to show that she'd actually seen it. My maths having been marked as Fail, my running away had seemed the logical conclusion – and, anyway, it's always the first option in cases involving missing children. Later on, when some kind of ransom note was expected, our phone was put on police intercept and my parents would jump every time it rang. At one point even my father was under suspicion. In the meantime, newspaper headlines told the story so far. 'SABINE: NO TRACE' 'HELICOPTER JOINS IN SEARCH FOR SABINE' 'POLICE BAFFLED'

A police incident centre was set up with a direct line for potential witnesses. Hastily printed posters were soon everywhere, pasted onto walls, shop windows or just handed out in the street. The river was dredged, the police carried out all the usual house-to-house enquiries, helicopters were used to scour the countryside and children from the local secondary school were even brought in to help search the surrounding wasteland, hacking their way through the undergrowth for clues. Hundreds of motorists stuck notices on their cars. In total, five hundred men and a hundred and sixteen soldiers were brought in to help. All in vain. The search continued for eighty days while that photo of me as a schoolgirl became part of the scenery, pasted on walls throughout Belgium and even abroad.

DISAPPEARANCE OF A MINOR
Height: 4′ 9″, slim build, blue eyes, shoulder-length fair hair. Last seen wearing black trainers (rope-soled), blue jeans, with a white top under a red jumper

and a light anorak (blue) around her waist. Sabine had her identity card with her and also her school satchel branded Kipling. She also had in her possession about 100 Belgian francs. She left home riding a bicycle, a Dunlop VTT, colour metallic green, with a red nylon bag secured behind the saddle. She was last seen on the Audenarde Road, close to the motorway underpass, headed in the direction of Tournai, around 07.20 am on 28 May 1996. If you have seen Sabine or believe you have information that could lead to her recovery, please contact the following number . . .

From then on I was just one in a desperate line of girls and young women who had been reported missing in Belgium:

Julie Lejeune and Melissa Russo. Missing (together) since June 1995, aged eight.

An Marchal and Eefje Lambrecks. Missing (together) since 23 August 1995, aged seventeen and nineteen.

Sabine Dardenne. Missing (alone) since 28 May 1996, aged twelve and a half.

Laetitia Delhez. Missing (alone) since 9 August 1996, aged fourteen and a half.

We were six victims of a crime that, like an earthquake, would shake my country to its political and institutional core and which journalists throughout the world, to this day, refer to simply as the Dutroux Case or the Monster of Belgium.

I lived it from the inside. And over the intervening years I have chosen to say nothing about my own 'case', the time I spent with the most hated psychopath in Belgium.

I am one of the rare survivors, a girl who was lucky enough to escape almost certain death at the hands of this type of killer. I decided to write this account so that people should understand, that there should be an end to all the strange looks, an end to the questions once and for all and for ever.

But if I have found the courage to retrace my stations of the cross, it has been, above all, so that lawyers should never again underestimate the damage paedophiles do, never again let them off with half their sentences still to run, never grant parole for 'good conduct' without other constraints in place. Some paedophiles are deemed to be intelligent, and psychologically responsible, making them suitable candidates, it would seem, for little more than the psychiatrist's chair. This attitude displays a terrifying naïvety.

The only thing that will work for these men is prison for a good long time. Or, in the case of serial offenders, life. It's what happens to the serial offenders that makes me really spit blood. There are now plenty of sophisticated tracking techniques capable of monitoring the movements of a 'predatory loner' once he's been identified. The law can provide the means, but it's down to governments to allow the follow-through.

Please, don't ever let them forget the future. Never again.

On 28 October 2004, I turned twenty-one. The future is waiting for me, and I have every hope that it will be a peaceful one, even if 'one can never forget the unforgettable'.

Sabine Dardenne
August 2004

CHAPTER 1

On my bike

I was twelve, and my bike had been a present from my god-father for my first Communion, by far the biggest and best present I'd got. He'd bought it from a shop in Mons, and it was a limited edition Dunlop Viking. It even had the number stamped on it, so it wasn't as if there were thousands like it. It was a beautiful shiny green colour, with yellow marks on the spokes. My father had had to change the lights as they weren't working properly, so he'd used the ones from my old bike. So all in all, it was pretty unique. I'd been using it to cycle to school ever since I'd got it, just a few weeks before. Every morning I'd put my satchel on my back, like a backpack, then strap the little zip-up bag where I kept my swimming things onto the carrier shelf behind the saddle, and then I'd be off, pedalling away just as the sun began to spread its light over the sky.

One Monday, 28 May 1996.

You don't spend every morning wondering if you're going to be snatched in mid-air by some madman in a camper van. Each time I've had to explain how it happened – first to the original investigators, then later in court, or to my best friend at the time – I see myself back there again, my bike being dragged alongside the high hedge, only fifty yards from my friend's garden. I am perfectly capable of taking the same route on foot, or by car, or by bike. But that place and time are stuck fast, unbearably and for ever, in my head. Because it was at that moment that my childhood was murdered.

That morning my father watched me leave, following me with his eyes to the point where the motorway underpass begins. I gave him a little wave, and then set off towards my school. Me going my way and he going his. Just after the underpass the road forks, and I had to make sure I went left, towards the stadium, then past the swimming pool, then on to school.

The whole journey took between ten minutes and a quarter of an hour. In terms of distance it was only about a mile and a half, two miles at the very most, so by the time I reached the stadium, I was about a third of the way there.

It's like a ghost road at that time of the morning. Not even a dog padding around. It must have been half past seven, and I'd left home no more than five minutes before. Often my friend Davina would wait for me in front of her house. Her parents' garage backed onto the road that ran past the stadium. She would watch for me to crest the hill from her garden and wave, and once I'd seen her, I'd wait for her to join me and then we'd go the rest of the way together, the two of us. In fact, sometimes we'd be three when her little brother would pedal along too. If I didn't catch up with her from the top of the rise, I would carry on by myself and catch up with her later at school. Because sometimes her mother took her by car – or she might just have got fed up with waiting and gone on without me. Or sometimes she was just running late.

On this particular morning I decided not to hang around. Once I got to school I still had to lock up my bike, which always took longer than you thought. She would understand. We knew how it worked, and it wasn't as if it was the first time we hadn't gone together.

So anyway, that morning, I saw from some way off that Davina wasn't there, and I just carried on riding down the empty road, along the thick high hedge the other side of the stadium. As the road there gets quite narrow, I'd always ride in the middle, and only when I heard an engine behind me would I pull over to let it pass. I always liked to get to school in good time to stow away my bike.

It was nearly the end of term – the end of my first year at secondary school, in fact. I hadn't done too badly, apart from maths. I was rubbish at maths and my mother was always getting at me to make more of an effort.

'Failed again, Sabine . . .'

9

I just let it wash over me, and would make my escape to the shed at the side of the garden, and either play there or sneak out to see one of my friends. I know that people had me down as a stroppy little madam, but as long as it didn't affect what I did, I wasn't bothered what they called me. In fact, I considered that this stroppy little madam was probably my best friend and this is still the case.

I wasn't necessarily thinking along those lines on that morning of 28 May 1996. I can't even remember if I was thinking at all. I was just pedalling along, minding my own business along a rather miserable road that ran beside the high wall of the football stadium.

When I heard an engine coming up behind me, I pulled over to the right, as usual. I had gone about fifty yards beyond Davina's garage, and I was right by the hedge. There was a house behind this hedge, and if someone had been standing at the window, or in the garden, they would have seen everything. But there was no one about; it was too early and still not quite light. If Davina had been waiting for me that morning, then none of this would ever have happened. Or if the school children who sometimes used this road as a cut-through had been there – I had seen them before – then at least there would have been dozens of witnesses.

But I saw no one. I was out in front.

It was a real old banger, the kind of beaten up camper van that looked as if it was lived in by squatters, three seats in the front and a miserable bunk thing in the back and disgusting brown and yellow check curtains, with hundreds of car stickers plastered all over the windows. Whenever I'd see one of these rust buckets when I was out with my mother I'd have a good laugh. 'Hey, Mum. I shouldn't get too close. Any minute now and that juddering heap of junk will explode and we'll be knocked unconscious by flying debris!'

I'd just had time to sense it coming up behind me, but saw it properly only when it was right beside me; the side door slid open, and a man leaning out, while another man was doing the driving. I didn't understand exactly what was happening, because instinctively at that point I closed my eyes, even before I felt afraid. It felt as if I'd been grabbed from off my bike, and the next second, I was literally swinging in mid-air, with one hand round my mouth and another covering my eyes. For a split second my foot got stuck under the saddle but then came free, leaving my bike careering on down the road on its own. In a flash I'd been thrown inside and my satchel wrenched off my back.

You see it in films. Images, flashing on the screen, one after the other. And then it's over. Done. And later, much later, when I was trying to explain how it had happened to Davina, all she kept saying was why hadn't I done anything? Couldn't I at least have tried to fight them off? But one moment I was pedalling, and the next moment I was inside the van.

It later turned out that they'd been tracking me for a week, like hunters. Of course I tried to fight them off, but I was half their size. A twelve-year-old who looked more like ten. 4′ 9″, and less than 5 stone. I was a bit of a sad case. 'Puny', the bullies at school had called me; they couldn't believe that I was old enough to be at secondary school at all.

The second I was in the van I'd been trussed up in a blanket, but when I caught sight of this man's hand about to shove some kind of pills into my mouth I began to yell at the top of my voice, so he pushed all his weight against me and growled at me to shut up.

'Just shut up and nothing will happen to you.'

But I had no intention of shutting up. I'd show this bastard.

'Who are you? What do you want?' I shouted. 'What do you think you're doing? And what about my bike? What have you done with it? Don't you understand? I'll be late for school. Who are you? Just let go of me! I'm on my way to school. What is it you want?' These questions had been pouring out of me right from the start, and I hate not getting answers. Even now, if I don't get an answer, I freak out, and I go on and on, relentlessly, until I get what I want. I suppose that my yelling was just instinct, a reflex action, until fear began to constrict my throat and I felt I was suffocating.

That one moment is undoubtedly the most violent I have ever experienced in my life. It was so sudden and so shocking that I was knocked utterly sideways. In just one second I had completely disappeared from the outside world – even though I didn't yet know it. I was in shock: the incredible speed of it, the terror of those black eyes inches from my face, and the hand trying to shut me up, this complete stranger with his weird accent, and then being trapped by that stinking blanket.

I felt the van stop, the sideways lurch as the driver got out.

'OK. Get the bike. And don't forget the bag. Now, hit it.' It was the man in the back doing the ordering. I heard the crunch of the gears and we were off again. My bike was now lying beside me, where it had been thrown by the driver. The red bag with my swimming things in it was there as well.

The whole thing – the snatching, the yelling, the stop, the flinging of my things into the van – had taken no more than a minute.

I already hated this creep with his horrible eyes, and his dirty greasy hair, oily enough to fry chips in, as we used to say. Not to mention his ridiculous moustache. He was a great ugly brute.

I was still struggling to get out of my blanket prison, yelling both with fear and rage, and he didn't like it at all.

'Just shut it!'

The truth was, of course, that pinned down by this blanket on top of an old mattress in the middle of the van, I could do absolutely nothing. The back of the driver's head was just visible above the head-rest, but he kept silent. I could tell, though, that compared with the creep, he was a bit on the small side, a real little nerd who'd do exactly what he was told. He was young, black hair, black jacket, pathetic hat complete with stupid badge. A real loser. It all went together: the dirty driver, the stinking van, the greasy creep. But what could they want with me? I never imagined for a moment that anything sadistic lay behind the kidnapping. I mean, if they'd been hovering outside the playground offering me sweeties, that would be one thing. But all I could think of was that these two animals must have something against me. Ripping me off my bike like that, it was obvious. Exactly what, I had no idea. It all seemed totally mad.

The first time I'd managed to spit out the pills he forced into my mouth. There must have been four or five of them, and I hid them under the mattress which stank of pee. Then they dabbed something on a tissue and pressed it into my face, some kind of ether, but I still kept on yelling.

'If you don't stop . . .' he threatened and I knew from his expression that I'd be hit. My mind was working overtime. 'Think,' I said to myself. 'If you carry on screaming and yelling, he's going to start using his fists. And that'll be worse. You've got to stay calm. Pretend to behave. If you start behaving then perhaps you'll find out exactly what it is that he wants. And why they're stopping you going to school.' In any case, by now I was feeling dizzy and I think I must have gone quiet for a bit. Not long enough for him, though. He forced me to swallow two capsules washed down with Coke, but I began to retch and these things refused to go down. I needed some more Coke, I said.

'You can't. The other one's had the lot.'

He called him 'the other one' because he didn't want to

say his name. I still didn't understand. Then I began to cry from sheer anger.

'Who are you? What do you want from me? I want to go home. My parents will be wondering what's happened and what are you going to tell them?'

He said nothing. But I kept on and on, asking the same questions, over and over again, never getting anything out of either of them in return. I just cried and cried, by now terrified out of my wits. And on it went, this rust bucket on wheels. Where to, I had no idea, though from the sound of the tyres we had been on a country road and now we were heading down a motorway.

In the end I decided that I would pretend to go to sleep, so I turned my back on the greasy creep and closed my eyes. With luck he'd think I was out for the count. All the time I was listening out for anything that they might say. But it was just road directions that the greasy creep was giving the other guy. 'That's it, turn here . . .' Somehow I had the feeling that they always knew perfectly well where they were, and how to get where they were actually going.

It was the greasy creep who was clearly in charge. Every so often I tried to work out where we might be going to, when I managed to catch a glimpse of a road sign. A few flashed by but meant nothing to me. My stomach was churning, worse even than before an exam. The sort of fear that makes you think you're going to pee in your pants because you're shaking so much. I don't know if they realised – they probably couldn't have cared less anyway – but as I lay there, I felt as if I was made of glass, and that any moment I could break in two. By now I was feeling really sick. I couldn't seem to swallow, as if something was stuck in my throat. It was difficult to breathe, I could feel myself panting like a dog, and I was still trying to make sense of it all: the disgusting blanket, the stinking mattress, the incessant rattling of the beaten up old banger, and my two companions with their weird accent, particularly the creep's. In Belgium, by the time you've reached the age of twelve, accents are easy to place. You can tell if someone comes from this town, or that. Sometimes it's just a question of how they roll their Rs. So because of that I would have said that they were Flemish speakers, coming from the north of the country towards the Dutch border, rather than French speakers from the south. But there was nothing specific. To me they just sounded like foreigners, stinking savages. The questions remained: 'Who are they?' and 'Where are they taking me?' and 'Why?'

As for an escape plan, I hadn't a hope in hell. First, we were speeding along, so any idea of climbing out of a window was pointless and in any case they were firmly closed and completely dark, thanks to those disgusting curtains and stickers plastered everywhere. The windscreen was the only place I could see daylight, which left the door at the back as the only real possibility. To get out that way I'd have to turn right round, and then just try to bash my head against the rusty metal. But I'd only have to move and they'd be on to me. And in any case, how long would I last on an open road, even running full pelt, assuming I hadn't already broken some bone? There was no way out. I pulled the blanket over my head, so that I could open my eyes without them noticing. They had to think that I was totally unconscious. But it was like an oven under that blanket, and it itched.

Although it was nearly the end of May, at the time I left for school in the morning, it was still quite cold, so I had on not only an ordinary top, but a jumper and my anorak as well. It wasn't that thick but I felt as if I was pouring with sweat, though it was more from fear and worry and from just not knowing what was going on. Although my body was immobile, it didn't stop my brain from churning. What should I have done? Carried on pedalling a bit longer? Thrown myself on the ground before they could grab me? I knew there was a little path that led off from the road, opposite the stadium. I could have just chucked my bike down on the ground, run up the path and hammered on the door of the first house I'd come to. But that hedge was so long. If only I hadn't taken my bike to school . . . Was it my fault? Was this some kind of punishment? I just couldn't believe what had happened. It was all so quick. I hadn't even had my feet on the ground. They'd snatched me in mid-air! And I saw nothing. Had the van been behind me all the time? Had they been following me?

The engine had stopped. The creep thought I was sleeping.

'We'll have to wake her up. Get her into the trunk when I give the word.'

When I saw what trunk they were talking about – a blue metal thing, all rusted over, no bigger than a tool box – the stroppy little madam decided to wake up.

'There's no way I'm getting in there.'

'Yes you are.'

'No I'm not. It's far too small.'

I was absolutely terrified. I've had problems with my lungs ever since I was little. I become short of breath very easily, and what with the fume-ridden old van and the hideous blanket, I was already nearly suffocating as it was. At the sight of this box fear completely took over. Fear of not being able to breathe, fear of not seeing where I was being taken.

So I continued to argue.

'It's too small. I won't be able to breathe in there. And it's disgusting. I'll get myself all dirty.'

As I showed no sign of budging, the creep called the other one over to help.

'We'll have to fold her up to get her in.'

I wasn't exactly fat, but even so. It wasn't easy and they could hardly close the lid. I was concertinaed into four, and they had to wait to the very last minute before shutting me in. I had no idea where they had brought me to, but the journey seemed to have gone on so long that it must have been miles and miles and miles. From the noises that I could hear through the metal, I tried to work out what they were doing. First they opened the van door, then lifted me out, putting the box on the ground. Then came the sound of another door opening.

18

The trunk was lifted up, then put down again. After about two minutes – which seemed for ever – they opened me up.

'Get out!'

Fear took hold of me once again. I'd become resigned to staying in the trunk. At least I was alone in there, dark though it was, locked in though I was. I didn't move.

Only the creep seemed to be there. The driver with the hat had disappeared, perhaps to get rid of another bit of my poor bike which has never been found. It probably got stolen. I thought later how it would have been covered with finger-prints as they weren't wearing gloves, so I hoped against hope that it would be found.

As I really had been folded into four, the creep had to pull me out. Not that I had any intention of doing anything to help him. I continued to pretend I was unconscious, adding realism to this charade by mumbling incoherently, 'What's happening? What's happening?'

I don't know if I was doing this play-acting wittingly or not. Though with hindsight I do wonder. Could it have been just instinct? A still vague idea that anything to make them less vigilant was worth doing, anything to get them off my back – and then, possibly, to find a moment . . . But I don't think I was consciously thinking like this at the time. It was more likely that the fumes from the van and the two capsules that I hadn't been able to spit out had played a part. I was clear-headed enough to see what was around me, however. Like my satchel.

There was only me and him now – a man without a name, in a ground-floor room of a house without a name. I wasn't really paying much attention to my surroundings – by which I mean the furniture and general decoration – but it struck me as being particularly unattractive. I noticed that there was a front door: closed. On the same side there was a window with the blind drawn right down, even though it was daytime, and I wondered why.

The details of that room eventually became imprinted on my memory, but only later. Perhaps by the third day . . .

The room was square. In one corner there were toys and a cot. The wall by the window was covered with cupboards and shelves filled with different kinds of stuff. In another corner there was a frying pan and a microwave. On the far wall a door, which apparently led to another room. The floor was covered with bricks, sacks of cement, tools, presumably to do with the half-built fireplace in the back wall. A sort of path had been cleared through the junk, and it led to another door – also enjoying a bit of DIY – blocked up by crossed planks of wood and plastic. I never found out where it led to. On another wall was a range of white kitchen cabinets that were empty. A staircase led to an upper floor. Beside the stairs was the fridge, quite big, with a telephone perched on top of it. Too high for me.

I worked that out pretty quickly. In the middle of this tip was a table and some chairs. I don't remember now whether I noticed, that first day, the other part of the staircase, the part that led down to the cellar. The only information I could glean from this room was that the place I now found myself in was not a normal house lived in by normal people.

I was desperately thirsty and asked for something to drink. The creep handed me a glass of milk which I drank straight down. The next thing I knew I was upstairs in a bedroom, the shutters closed. I have no idea how I got there, by myself or if I was carried. I have only the memory of obeying orders, of doing what I was told.

He said I was to get undressed, and to get into one of the bunk beds. So I did. I'd asked so many questions and cried so much during the journey that I had no more strength left other than to obey. I was probably paralysed with fear and my head all drugged. I must have found it very odd lying down with nothing on in this strange, dark room with just a blanket on top of me. No sooner had I done what I was told than he put a chain around my neck which he then padlocked to the ladder leading to the top bunk. He put a chamber pot beside it. My chain was about three feet long, just enough to let me reach this pot.

I preferred to stay there, without moving, hidden under the blanket, staring at the ceiling. High in one of the walls there was a little window that let in a tiny amount of light. I can no longer remember whether he brought me anything to eat. In any case I couldn't have swallowed it. Perhaps I slept, exhausted from all that crying. But I can still hear myself saying 'Why am I here? This chain hurts. I can hardly breathe.

I'm not an animal, you know.' The curtains were closed and there was no light in the room. However, I had glanced at my watch when I'd got here. It said half past ten. The journey here had therefore taken at least two hours. But where was 'here'? Too far, in any case.

On one wall there was a poster of a dinosaur. I'd forgotten that dinosaur . . . Strange, considering how long it had irritated me – to the point where I couldn't stand it. Here I was, chained to this child's bed. There was a baby's cot downstairs. And toys. So at some time there must have been children in this house. My brain churned away in the dark, trying to get to grips with my strange new environment. What was I doing there? And what would happen to me now?

The second day, the creep came into the room, squatted down beside the bed and then began to tell me a horrendous story.

'You're not to worry. Personally I've got nothing against you. In fact I saved your life. But the boss really has it in for you. So he wants money from your parents.'

On the third day, to give his story added punch, he brought in 'the other one', the nerd in the hat, who just agreed with what the creep said in monosyllables, his limited repertoire being 'yes', 'That's true', 'Yes, that's it'. After which the creep with the moustache would say, 'You see? I'm not the only one. Just listen to him. He says it too.'

He then told me that the boss had it in for me because my father, who had been in the police, had done a 'bad thing'. So this boss was bent on vengeance, and the plan was to get at my father through one of his children. Which turned out to be me. He would be demanding a ransom, either one or three million. At least that's what I thought, but now, remembering how I'd said '*phfff*' when I heard the money they were talking about, I realise it must have been three. One million, at a pinch, my parents might have been able to get their hands on by borrowing from everyone in sight. But three! Even if they sold the house, the car – everything they possessed – I knew it was completely out of the question.

How did they know that my father had been in the police before he changed jobs? Was it me? Had I told them in that way you do when you're a child? 'You better watch out, 'cause my dad's a policeman . . .'

It's perfectly possible. In any case, this rigmarole they'd invented was based around that. The 'bad thing' that my father was supposed to have done wasn't clear in my mind. Had he punished the boss by putting him in prison? Did he owe him money? Here I was, a prisoner because of it, and now they were trying to get him to pay a ransom. That at least had been clear from day one. I tried to defend my parents.

'But they don't have that kind of money. They're not millionaires.'

The creep made me understand that it would have to be 'worked out'. Somehow. Because otherwise . . . I was dead meat.

It's hard to recall now exactly what happened when, and

in what order. But I think that it was at this stage that the 'interference' started. On the second day my head was a bit clearer and, having removed the chain, the creep led me through to another bedroom next door, which appeared to be his, with a double bed, which I later named the Calvary* room. It was there that I was forced to put up with this man doing things to me. I know that he also took some Polaroids. Before or after, it's difficult to say as I only realised what he was doing after the second or third flash. It seemed so strange. I mean, why did he need to photograph me naked and chained to this bed? I can still remember my reaction.

'Wasn't it any good then?'

I never stopped crying, and this really got to him. He seemed to think that I should've enjoyed it . . . Afterwards I'd be taken back to the other bedroom to be reattached to the bunk and told to go to sleep.

Even now I can't really understand how I could bear this man, this disgusting ugly, stinking old man (after all, that's what he was in my twelve-year-old eyes) doing these things to me. I was being held for ransom, I understood that. But this? He claimed that he had saved my life, while at the same time he continued to treat me like an animal. It's true that, up until then, I hadn't actually been hit or beaten, or raped. Yet his behaviour was so disgusting that I just had to try hard not to think about it, just empty my mind of the vileness of it all.

I'd find myself back in my bunk, chained up, my eyes on

* Calvary in French also means agony.

24

the ceiling, once again paralysed by fear, with just one idea chasing its tail in my head: What next? What's going to happen to me next? This 'next' was terrifying enough, before anything actually happened. I spent my time crying, dozing off from time to time. I had a permanent headache, I was in a state of shock. Utterly without hope, and alone. Worse than any nightmare anyone could possibly imagine.

The trap began to close around me. The brainwashing continued, although I had no idea that's what it was. The creep then told me that my parents had refused to pay my ransom, even the police had refused to pay. (Was that because my father had been in the police?) I was therefore in grave danger, because the boss had decided I would have to be 'liquidated'.

Then, suddenly the monster with the greased-down hair transformed himself into my saviour.

'Look, I had to do what I was told.' He meant: kidnap me. 'I had no choice: just following orders from the boss. But as your parents won't cough up, you can't stay here, or he'll kill you. So what happens is up to you. Do you want to live or die?'

I can't be sure of the exact phrase, but what he offered was a stark choice. Live or die. Naturally, I chose to live.

'Okay. But then I'll have to hide you. I'll say that you're dead, but you'll still be alive and I'll look after you. Obviously I can't leave you here, in this room, because the boss would see you. These are his headquarters, you see, so he could turn up here at any moment. And if you had any idea about running away, well, he'd get you back just in order to kill you. A matter of honour. All the houses around here are under his command, so it's a bit of a tricky one. But I know a place, a secret place, where I could hide you.'

Headquarters? So were these people gangsters? The police? Soldiers? Aliens? My head was going round and round. And always, that question gnawing away at the bottom of it all: Who is this man? This creep who dragged me off my bike, doing horrible things to me that I didn't like one bit. First he talks about wanting money off my parents, next he's taking pictures of me without clothes on. He chains me up, unchains me. It's not normal for a girl of my age to be the girlfriend of someone like this. But to die? I could never have chosen to die! In my head I had to stick with this hope, day after day, that I would go on living.

After these three days were up, he took me down into his 'secret place'.

CHAPTER 2

The scenario

I couldn't bring myself to admit that I had been well and truly kidnapped. The word just refused to surface. The whole thing had been too well done, too quick – right from the first day while I was still stupefied with fear and my head muddled with drugs, so I had believed everything I was told. This man was 'my saviour', and he had made me believe this machiavellian scenario: that thanks to him, I had escaped the clutches of someone even more monstrous than himself, this boss of who-knew-what, who wanted to kill me. In order for that not to happen, I had to obey the every whim of this ogre who'd appeared out of thin air, suffer his fiddling around with me in order just to survive, to live. Hidden by him, and with him. For how long?

Sometimes, in films, gangsters kidnap the child of a police

officer and then demand a ransom. And you think: it's only a film. Things like this don't happen in real life. Or at least, they might happen to other people, but not to anyone you might know, particularly anyone like you. And now, here I was, in precisely that kind of scenario. Me. Sabine, a first-year at the local secondary school. And the person chained up to this bed? None other than me as well, hidden somewhere in the bowels of the headquarters of a sinister gangland organisation whose boss had the power to have me killed for the flimsiest of reasons, let alone for trying to escape.

'You were lucky it was me,' the creep would say, 'because the boss, now, he couldn't give a toss whether you lived or died.'

'Lucky' that it was 'him'. But who was this 'him'? He never told me his name, and, as for 'the other one', he'd done a complete vanishing act. Once his few lines were out of the way, so was he. I never saw the nerd or his stupid hat again.

Once, I actually asked him, the creep, that is, 'So what's your name then?'

I had a choice, he told me. I could call him either Alain or Marc. After that I decided I preferred him to be anonymous and never called him anything but 'you'. As in: 'Please would you give me back my clothes?' I was fed up with always being naked and didn't want to have to go downstairs to eat with nothing on.

I hated not wearing clothes. I was always cold and I didn't see the point of it. So I carried on badgering till eventually he

28

gave them back. First I got my underwear and then my jeans. Or perhaps it was the other way round. All I do know is that I went for weeks wearing the same knickers. And only knickers. It was so hard to keep track.

I knew that I'd been kidnapped on Monday 28 May. The first three days, before going down to the 'secret place' and before I began to get over whatever drug it was I'd been forced to swallow, things still weren't too clear, so there was really nothing to help me gauge the time. So many weird things would happen, even in the course of a single day. I'd go downstairs to eat. Then it would be upstairs again for another photo session, then on to the other things, which I took to calling his 'circus' because I knew no other way of thinking of his fiddling around with me. And all the time I was being fed all these stories about the mighty boss. I never stopped asking myself questions about what was happening but it was all so unreal that, even when I looked at my watch which told me what day it was, I had the feeling that I'd been locked up in this stinking hovel for ever.

At the end of the third day, he takes me down into his 'secret place', the 'hidy-hole'. There's a staircase leading down to a cellar, and I see a shelf that seems to come out of the wall as if by magic, and I think I must be hallucinating. On this stack of metallic shelving there are packs of bottled water, packs of beer, and other different kinds of bottles. The first thing he does is take everything off and put it on the floor. Then, grabbing hold of the lowest shelf, he pulls it towards him – and a whole piece of the wall opens up. Then he wedges open this invisible door, which must have weighed half a ton, with a concrete brick, leaving only a small triangular gap to squeeze behind. Once the shelf is back in place, it's completely invisible. When he shows me how it works I can tell he's really quite proud of his handiwork. The first bit of the hidy-hole, just behind the false door, strikes me as being more like a glory-hole – a mess of cardboard, paper, bits of metal, but he says I am forbidden to go rootling around in it. Needless to say, at the first opportunity I have to rootle, I do.

When you edge over to the right, you come to a gate like a metal grille, which was always open. Immediately after that there's a sort of bed base made of wooden slats, with a mattress on top of it, like something you might find in a skip, falling apart. Disgusting.

It was quite a narrow cellar, about three feet wide and nine feet long. (I didn't actually measure it myself – I found out later.) But I didn't need measurements to realise that I could suffocate in this place. It was so dank and dirty that one look was enough.

There was a little wooden shelf fixed to the wall, two light bulbs, and a small plank that couldn't take anything very much, but this was where I used to keep my crayons and my glasses. At the far end of the wall, where the head of the bed went – if you can call something so hideous a bed – was another shelf, high up, with an old television on it that did duty as a video screen, and a Sega game console. On the wall to the right was a little bench and table. If I sat on the bench, then my feet were on the mattress. At the end of the mattress was the grille, and then the concrete door with the glory-hole off to the side. At the bottom of the bed there was just enough room to put my satchel and the chamber pot.

You turned the TV on by pressing a knob. It was so ancient that he must have got it off a skip. There was no remote – it was all wooden fascia and knobs. Needless to say, it didn't work. It was only used for playing the game.

He had given me the impression that he'd constructed this dirty little hole specially for my benefit. Looking at the tacky wooden bed base and the decrepit TV screen, it should have been obvious to me that I wasn't the first occupant. But he went on about how he'd had to do it up very quickly, especially for me. It was such a dump that I believed him. The bit of the hidy-hole that was mine had been painted – sloshed would be a better word – a hideous yellow colour. A two-year-old could have done a better job. The walls were concrete and the place had originally been a water cistern.

So I'm going to be shut up in this hell-hole. I remember making a face as if to say 'You've got to be joking'. To pacify me, he demonstrated the state-of-the-art ventilator he'd installed. It was a pathetic thing that had once been part of a computer, and was now attached to the roof.

31

'This way you won't have a problem with lack of air,' he explained.

Then the false half-ton door closed upon me. And I still had no answers to my questions. Why me? Why here? Why had my parents given up on me? Why did he need me for his 'circus'? I cried so much that I could hardly breathe.

I needed a structure, a routine, something to hang on to. How was I going to wash myself? How was I going to empty the chamber pot? What was I going to do all the time on my own? How was I going to stay sane? I had my watch, an exercise book from school, my French homework, a couple of textbooks, my felt tips and pencils, some loose-leaf paper from a ring-binder and a stupid pocket video game. There was this little man and you had to get him to jump over stones to amass points. If he came across a mushroom he got bigger, if he came across a fireball, he had to shoot fireballs. I'd borrowed it from a friend of mine. I'd first played it at her house, but had never been able to get beyond Level 1. By Level 2 land had become water, which was much more difficult and I always messed up. So I was stuck at Level 1, which I must have done at least a hundred times and which drove me mad.

Just before he left me, he told me he was going to bring me down some emergency supplies, in case he couldn't come himself for any reason. These emergency supplies turned out to be cartons of milk, jerrycans of tap water and bread. I never imagined for a moment that I would spend the rest of my life in this hell-hole. I still believed that my parents would come up with something, pay the ransom somehow. Because, of course, that was the deal. Even though I hadn't a clue how they could ever get hold of that kind of money. I had no idea either that, while I was stuck down here like a rat in a trap, the whole of Belgium was going mad looking for me. He, of course, had told me that my parents knew exactly what had happened. Nothing was happening simply because they couldn't – or wouldn't – come up with the cash. This monster had somehow succeeded in convincing me, little by little, that I had been abandoned, and that I was lucky to have him to watch over me, like some kind of hideous guardian angel, and that my parents knew full well what the situation was, and that the ball was now entirely in their court. Slowly but surely, 'They can't pay' had become 'They won't pay'. And the final desperate conclusion: For whatever reason, your parents haven't paid. They probably think that you are dead.

From then on, life in this pit followed the same pattern: First of all I wasn't allowed to cry or make any noise. The boss, or God knows who else, could come into the house at any time, he said. Safety equalled silence. I had the Sega game, my satchel and school things, and that would have to be enough to keep me busy. Every time he came to get me, to take me upstairs – either to get something to eat or to do the 'other things' – I'd hear him first from the other side of the concrete wall saying, 'It's me'. If it wasn't his voice, he said, then I had to stay absolutely still and absolutely quiet. My life depended

33

on it. Literally. Because any time I protested – which I did all the time – he'd warn me that 'It'll be worse for you with the boss'.

'Worse' meant torture, in that the boss wouldn't just use his body to force me to do what he wanted, oh no. He had other things at his disposal, the ultimate, of course, being death. I was terrified. Every moment of every day. Even when I was alone in the hole, it was as if I was in some terrible race, trying to outrun Death, who was always just behind my shoulder. My brain just churned, going over and over the same old ground. What else was there to do? I'd think, 'This time he's gone to fetch his friends, and when they get back, they're going to kill me.' If I ever dared to say no to something, I was terrified that he would beat me up or even murder me. Though after a while, I realised that he wouldn't ever hit me himself, it was only threats. And he barely needed to open his mouth; those evil black eyes spoke for themselves. I knew it would only take a nod, and the boss, or another member of the gang, would take over and do the dirty work for him.

Sometimes I wondered whether keeping me here was really his idea after all, and when he got bored with me, or fed up with my general stroppiness, he'd just get rid of me. This threat hung over me like an axe every waking moment.

Whenever I took to feeling sorry for myself, banging on about how my parents seemed to be doing nothing to get me out, he would tell me to count my blessings, to consider myself lucky just to be alive. And he would remind me that the boss had this whole range of torture instruments. Nor did he spare me details of how they would be used. They could be anything from a stick to a bottle to things so horrible they don't bear thinking about.

'You don't get it, do you,' he would shout. 'The boss doesn't give a shit about you. If he had any idea that you were still alive, he'd do far worse things than I could ever come up with!'

Somehow I managed to retain a certain dignity and a degree of authority. It was important to me, even though I knew that I would never have the last word. Occasionally, when he told me to do something, I would say, 'No, not that', knowing perfectly well that I had no real option, and that a minute or two later I'd have to do it anyway. I'd start off by being stubborn, but when I realised that I wasn't achieving anything, then I'd have to give in. In the long run it was better to do what he wanted. The alternative – the fear of being beaten or handed over to the boss – was too terrifying. Fear was my real ruler.

I decided to start a calendar, first in my exercise book, then on one of the loose-leaf pages. I started it on the 13th of June, because that was the last day of term and therefore I knew it was a Thursday. I had been locked up with this monster since Monday 28 May. Three days upstairs, then, on Friday 31 May, I began my subterranean life.

Between 31 May and 13 June – the date I started the calendar – my memories of exactly what went on are a bit vague as I really had nothing to hang them on to. He'd arrive to take me upstairs to get something to eat, then it was bedroom activities, then back to the hole again. A never-ending circle. Every day. And it hurts me to have to go through it: that hole was truly hell, Calvary, with the television, where he watched his fuzzy porn films on a satellite channel.

'Just look at that! Amazing!', he'd say.

'Yes, amazing,' I'd reply. Although I'd watched nothing at all. I just thought it was all stupid. And I would wait until he'd finished 'putting himself through his paces', which was my personal code for what he did. Sometimes I was relieved to go back to the cellar. Sometimes I was relieved to go upstairs, even though I knew all I could expect was more of 'his paces'. At least up there I wasn't suffocating down in the hole, where I could hardly move between the pot and my satchel. I seemed to breathe better upstairs, plus there was more to look at. For example, he had vast hanging rails full of clothes, women's and children's. But when I asked him if he was married, he said no. Any children, then? No.

When I complained about my own clothes, or lack of them, he generously off-loaded a pair of shorts (very short) and a minuscule T-shirt. When I asked if I could have a wash, he said only if he washed me himself, and then only once a week. If I wanted to feel even vaguely clean, I had no option but to endure his particular version of personal hygiene.

Whenever I was upstairs, I also got a sense of whether it was night or day, either from tiny shafts of light that came in through the gaps in the curtains, or from the window high up in the wall which was uncovered.

As for what I had to eat, it was rubbish. While he had cocoa, I had milk. For me he would heat up this horrible stuff in the microwave, while he'd fry himself a steak. He'd even eat chocolate right under my nose. I had a knife and fork, but what use were they when I couldn't even swallow? I would sit there, thinking about the fork in my hand, and what I could do with it . . . wondering where would be the best place to shove it. I would look at the front door; sometimes there'd even be a key sticking out of the lock. But he was always there between it and me. Even if I had managed to get out, I knew perfectly well he'd have grabbed me back within seconds. And that wasn't even counting what lay in wait for me. After all, I was right in the heart of the boss's headquarters. All the houses round about either belonged to him or were under his command. I think the creep must have had an idea of the way I was beginning to think, because after a while he decided that we should eat in the next room.

Very occasionally there'd be a ring at the front door when I was eating with him. Not often – two or three times, maybe. But I never saw who it was, nor what happened. He'd open the door, and then go out, only for a second or two.

'Just one of the gang,' he'd say when he got back. 'Nothing to worry about.'

I wasn't allowed to ask questions, and above all I wasn't allowed to make any noise – the reason, of course, being the possible proximity of the famous boss. Since I'd started eating in the other room, he'd taken to closing the connecting door so that I wouldn't be seen.

One day he showed me the stock of drugs that he kept in a plastic bag. He took them all out and piled them up according to type. This was his own little medicine chest, he explained. At one moment he made out as if he were a doctor: intelligent, knowing everything there was to know about anything medical. Then he made me admire his half-finished fireplace, which he considered a masterwork, a thing of beauty. So was he an architect then? There were even designs, things he'd done himself, or so he claimed, but I hardly remember them, as I had no intention of giving them more than a passing glance. Buildings of some kind anyway.

I had no idea how to place him, or any idea who he might have been, what he might have done, in real life. He claimed to be thirty, but I knew he was older. He claimed to have seven houses, all guarded by dogs, though he didn't have a garden. No wife either, because that wasn't the way the boss liked things, he explained, and he'd been with the gang for so long . . . He bored me rigid with his stories about the bloody boss, and the bloody gang, so mysterious and dangerous. It was fear that kept me believing all this gangster-movie stuff. But no doubt I bored him rigid too with my questions: 'When could I leave? When would I see my parents again?' And demands: 'I need a pillow to sleep. I need an alarm clock. I need different food, I'm fed up with milk, I need to wash my clothes, I need some paper to draw on. I need a toothbrush.' He gave me such a strange look when I asked about the toothbrush that I began to suspect it was something he rarely bothered to do himself.

When I was banging on like this, there would come a point when he'd just punch his fist down on the table and tell me to 'Shut the fuck up'. And I could tell, just by looking at him, that he was capable of much, much worse. It was all very strange. Sometimes he'd chat away perfectly normally, other times he'd totally lose it without any real reason. For example, if I refused to eat bread that had gone mouldy, or drink milk that had curdled, then he'd just go mad, because he'd bought it himself and he considered it my fault that they had gone off.

I hated his horrible accent, and him being such a know-all. And how could a saviour feed me so badly? Everything was so upside down. Instinctively, I knew that nothing really hung together, but I was only twelve, and just not capable of working out how the different pieces of the jigsaw might fit together. For example, why couldn't he at least let me telephone my parents? Because, he said, the line had to be kept open so that they could call us when they got the money. Also, this same telephone on top of the fridge was a hotline to the boss. The boss, who was richer than the prime minister and who had children. Everything in the house belonged to him, that I knew. And if I dared to use the telephone, then I'd be sure to get the boss, or another member of the gang, and then they'd realise that I was still alive . . .

39

At the beginning I'd thought about just calling 999 and asking them for help, but as this was the boss's hotline, it probably didn't even have a 999. And, anyway, I wasn't even tall enough to reach it. But just like the key in the door, and the fork, the idea of the telephone at least got my brain working.

My only defence was to run rings around him with my badgering, because once I'd got something in my sights, I wouldn't let go. I'd make my demands in the sort of voice that stands no nonsense and doesn't expect the answer no. I practised being cunning, never for a moment considering him as anything more than a stupid idiot.

Boredom and loneliness began to get to me. He gave in over the radio alarm clock, so at least I could now listen to music, though I couldn't get a news channel. I tried to fiddle with it, to get a signal that would allow me to hear something of the outside world, but it was no good. The foam mattress was by now crumbling away and there were insects everywhere.

Occasionally I imagined myself going through the wall: I'd attack it with the game console. I'd watch the clock like a maniac. I even made a list, so that each number of minutes could remind me of something else. 13.23: 23 is the number of our house, 29 is where my grandma lives. 17, my mother's birthday, 22 my father's birthday. One o'clock. I just stared, obsessed by hours and minutes and any numbers associated with them that came into my head, even down to shoe sizes.

These minute-numbers, and the non-minute associations, were all I had to give me hope. As I couldn't talk to anyone else, I talked to myself: 'Okay, I think I'll have a glass of water now.' 'Yes, well about time I had a look at my Dutch homework.' 'I'll just get my notebook and do a bit of work on that: maths, French, Latin, science. I looked at my school report, which should have been handed in, had been signed and, of course, my appalling maths marks. If I really attacked my maths, then I might just get through. In all my other subjects I was okay and I wasn't too worried about the maths because I'd heard there'd been a change in the rules, so you no longer had to pass every subject to move up to the next class. You just went up automatically. So there was no need to knock myself out any more over maths. I tried to work through the textbook on my own, but it was just too difficult. At least it kept me occupied.

Apart from that, I didn't really do much work as such. I had a Dutch vocabulary and grammar book, so I copied out a whole lot of words, but without bothering to actually understand them. I was like a machine. I also copied out some French quotations, copying and copying, filling up whole sheets of the loose-leaf pages with this stuff. And then I'd demand more paper for my drawings. I had no intention of using what was left of my own beautiful paper.

There was nothing I didn't miss. At home we had really nice food, I had my bed, and the little pillowcase that my grandma had made for me, and which I never went anywhere

41

without. Clean sheets, clean clothes, all my little bits and pieces. And Sam, my dog. My goldfish, Tifi. My little shed in the garden, my friends who must be wondering where on earth I'd got to. And how had my parents been able to explain why I hadn't been in to school?

I can't remember now whether I was the one who asked if I could write to my parents, or if it was his suggestion, for the sake of a bit of peace. But on Thursday 13 June, I wrote my first letter. I know because I marked it on my calendar. I wanted my parents to know exactly how things were in my temporary place of residence.

Unfortunately this letter has disappeared, if he even kept it in the first place, though three of the later ones have been found, so it is always possible.

On Friday 21 June he told me he was 'off on a mission'. These 'missions' had nothing to do with me, apparently. He'd already told me that the boss was always sending him to other places, even to the East. The good news was that I was spared the regular trips upstairs. The bad news was that I was locked up, totally alone, in my dank and dirty hell-hole. I couldn't bear the dark, so I left the big light on day and night, and I watched the clock radio as if I was a madwoman. I didn't make much of a hole in the emergency provisions he had so thoughtfully provided as it was mostly tinned stuff, like tomatoes and meatballs, which I would have to eat cold. 'Just drink the juice,' was his advice after I had complained. And of course there was the mouldy bread. But I made up for this by devouring little biscuits, called Nic-Nacs, in the form of letters of the alphabet. In fact they were about the only thing I did eat.

I think it might have been around this time that I began fiddling with the clock radio in the hope of getting some news of the outside world. Anything to link me somehow to my previous life. It wasn't that I thought they might be talking about me. I hadn't disappeared. No one was looking for me. To the best of my knowledge I had never heard of any missing girls in Belgium. And yet, I know now that I had seen a poster when I'd been round at a friend's house. Two little faces: Julie and Melissa, who disappeared on 24 June 1995, and whom no one had heard of since. A whole year before! I'd seen the poster, that was all. I made no connection between them and me. And yet . . . that horrible yellow paint was probably covering up sad traces of their presence before the new tenant arrived on the scene. I was completely oblivious of the upheaval outside, the state my parents must have been in, the posters that described me, like the other little girls, as 'missing' and gave my description. My height, my blue eyes, my fair hair, my build, even a photo of a bike exactly like mine, right down to a little red bag of swimming things behind the saddle.

They had been looking for me since the beginning. I knew nothing about the searches, the dogs, the probing along the river banks, everything that my parents had done, relentlessly and obstinately, never giving up, in order to find me.

*

On 26 June he was back. I had now been there thirty days. I assumed, rightly, that the Calvary-room performance would now be resumed. Upstairs, on that bed, he would attach himself to me with a chain that went around my ankle. Occasionally I had to 'sleep' next to him all night. But I never dared go to sleep, always terrified that he'd start doing his things while I was out cold and that, not being awake, I wouldn't even be able to say: 'No. I don't want to.' I felt every movement. The chain sawed into my ankle every time he rolled over in his sleep. Sometimes this stupid idiot even put it on the wrong ankle, putting his right foot with my right foot, so it was impossible for me to move any distance away from him, which obviously I always tried to do. The nights were long. I'd stare up at the ceiling, and – if he'd left it switched to a half-watchable programme – look at the television. Even if I did manage to close my eyes, or move to try and find a more comfortable position, I knew that I mustn't go to sleep. 'If he does anything, then at least you'll be able to fight him off.' This was the only vestige of honour I had left. Showing him that I refused. Saying 'No'. Rejecting him. Until the threats started, and I could no longer struggle.

To help myself stay awake, I would imagine what it was like at home: my mother coming back from work, my sisters watching television – they might even be watching the same thing as me. I thought about Sam, about Tifi, about my patch of garden and the seeds I had planted. I thought about my godmother's apple tart, my granny's pillowcase. And I thought, too, about how not to die of sheer boredom in the hole. How to drive this bastard next to me round the bend. If only I had some sort of weapon, like a knife to kill him with. What if I could chuck something at his head, like one of the bricks that were all over the floor downstairs? But what good would one brick be against his thick head? And, anyway, I was too little even to pick one up off the ground.

So I did what I could. From time to time I yanked on the chain, just to annoy him. I moaned at him to add some more links to make it more comfortable. I complained about everything. I went on about my parents endlessly. I wanted to telephone, to write. I even told him I wanted the TV Guide. I did everything I could to make life unbearable for him, to make him reel from being bombarded with recriminations and tears, and it seemed that I did get somewhere, even with only these pathetic measures at my disposal.

No TV Guide. No telephone. But some days I was allowed an extra link in the chain around my ankle. This wasn't enough to satisfy me, however, let alone help get me out of there. I tried to be as cunning as I could. I considered him an arsehole, which was the worst form of abuse our playground ran to.

Sometimes, when he insisted that I do something I didn't want to, I would call him names out loud, which at least did me good. 'You're an arsehole!' I'd shout. 'It's not normal what you do and I don't like it. You're just a shit!' Sometimes I had to use words like these, just to get the filth out of me. But it didn't seem to bother him – most of the time he couldn't have cared less, or else it put him into a temper, and he did what he was going to do anyway. So I didn't use this technique very often, and I reminded myself that my resistance could only go so far. Otherwise I could be in for a nasty shock.

But when we were eating, sitting opposite each other, the idea of shoving my fork someplace where it would hurt would come back to me. Or maybe throwing the frying pan straight at his face after he'd been chomping away on one of his steaks, while I'd been gagging on rancid mince made from infected meat.

When he told me to bring him a cup of coffee that he'd been reheating in the microwave, I was never allowed any. He'd only to move his fat bum to get it himself. 'I am not the maid,' I'd screech. 'Get it yourself. The microwave is three yards away!'

My stomach was knotted up with fear. I was sick of being on my own, of the shame, and the squalor. I was always short of breath, I had a permanent headache and my eyes were forever red from crying day and night.

I wanted him to know just how much he disgusted me. I knew nothing about what he called 'sex'. I had no idea, either, that people could be obsessed by it. No one had ever talked to me about that kind of thing. I hadn't yet started my periods. I'd never had a boyfriend. I had never even been kissed. Even so, I knew that what he was doing was not normal. He was old. I was twelve. And he spent his time making my life a misery with his weird behaviour. Who was this creep? All I could come up with was 'arsehole'.

I was naïve. Because there was much worse to come.

CHAPTER 3

Holding on

One day I noticed that 'the man looking after me' (as I called him in my letters) was reading a magazine my father used to get occasionally, *Science and Life*. And I remembered a special issue they'd had, all about the planets, which I'd really enjoyed, because I love anything to do with space. Anyway, I asked if I could borrow it.

'Come with me,' he said. 'I've got a whole lot of them in the attic.'

I took as many as he would let me, enough to last at least two days I reckoned; playing Sega all the time was really getting on my nerves. Sometimes, down there in the hole, I would go twenty-four hours without sleeping, sometimes I'd just collapse in a heap for twelve hours at a time. Sometimes, when the stress just got to me, and I was at my wits' end, I needed something to concentrate on that would stop me from going completely round the bend.

So it was there, in this magazine, that I saw a subscription form, filled out in the name of Michèle Martin, 128 Phillipeville Road, Marcinelle. In another issue I spotted the words 'Cell 154'.

A few days later, I was watching as he opened his post. We were sitting at the table, and with him opposite me I couldn't really see very well, and what I could read was upside down. I didn't dare make it obvious what I was doing, so I began to fool about, jerking my head around, pretending to be a bit gormless, just so as I could make out the address. And success! The postcode was the same as I'd seen on the subscription form: 6001. The house number was also the same: 128.

I had to concentrate really hard to get the name. It wasn't easy because he kept shuffling the envelopes about. But then, there it was, as clear as the moustache on his ugly face, Marc Dutroux. And exactly the same address in Marcinelle as I'd seen in *Science and Life*. The cogs were whirring now, and suddenly it fell into place. The names: when I'd asked what he was called he'd said Alain or Marc.

I'd told him I preferred Alain, as that was the name of a really nice hairdresser we used to go to, whereas Marc reminded me of a particularly nasty boy who lived on our estate and who was always kicking other people's balls. Not that it made any difference, because I could never bring myself to call him anything at all. To me he was just 'you'.

But now at least I knew where I was: 128 Phillipeville Road in Marcinelle, wherever that was. And this bastard's name was Marc Dutroux. I asked if he'd ever been in prison – I'd seen that cell number, remember – and he said yes, he had.

'For a long time?'

'Far too long,' he replied with a horrible expression. 'But don't you worry, I'm getting my own back. Judges and cops can go fuck themselves. Their laws mean nothing to me. I do whatever I want, and they haven't a cat in hell's chance of getting me this time.'

Where Marcinelle actually was, I hadn't a clue. It didn't ring any bells at all. If the address had been somewhere around Charleroi, I'd have had a better idea. But at least I knew now I was in Belgium. In Belgium postcodes are organised geographically and so, when I compared it with our own, I knew I couldn't be that far from our house. If only I knew exactly what time they had snatched me, and what time I got here . . . I wound my memory back to that morning of 28 May.

Twenty-five past seven, say half past seven, when they dragged me off my bike. Half past ten when I looked at my watch, after he'd chained me to the bunk. And say we'd got to the house an hour before that. So two hours to get here.

It was then that I began to think about the telephone again. I'd been aware of it from the very first day. And each time when I left my dungeon and came up to get something to eat, I'd see it, on my left, up there on top of the fridge, like a beacon.

'So, does the phone work then?'

'Not for you it doesn't. It's the headquarters hotline.'

'But if I could just talk to my parents for five minutes . . .'

'No. Their phone will be being tapped, so the boss will get to hear and you'll be killed.'

'They won't say anything,' I pleaded. 'I won't tell them where I am, or who's with me, or anything. I just want to see if they're all right.'

'No!'

The next time I tried another tack.

'Just two minutes . . . not even five . . . just two minutes . . .'

'No! If the boss, or someone else in the gang finds out that you're not dead, then there'll be real trouble.'

As the days dragged by, I became increasingly obsessed by this idea of phoning home. It wasn't as straightforward as just finding a way to get up there and dial. I'd been told that the telephone was a direct line to the boss, this man who wanted me dead. And I'd swallowed this story like chocolate buttons.

The first time I heard the hotline rigmarole, I was truly frightened. Of course I wouldn't phone. But as time went on, seeing it up there on top of the fridge just got to me. The most frustrating thing was knowing that he was using it without any apparent problem. Once I heard him say 'Miche' and make kissing noises down the phone.

'So, was that your girlfriend then?' I asked. 'I heard you sending kisses . . .'

'Mind your own business. I don't have a girlfriend.'

I heard him say the name 'Michel' several times, but I couldn't work out whether it was a man or a woman. Much later, after the trial, I found out that there were at least three Michels involved. Michèle his wife, Michel the nerd in the hat, and another Michel, his accomplice in his stolen-car business and other dodgy dealings (who was later acquitted of any involvement in the rapes and murders).

This was in the days before cordless phones so, as soon as he saw me watching, he'd go behind the fridge so that I wouldn't hear as much, or he'd put his hand over the receiver and tell me to stop listening, and to get on with eating my horrible food.

There was never much time for eating. Sometimes I'd be up and back down again within half an hour. Sometimes, if he'd decided on going through 'his paces', he'd take me up to the bedroom and then, well, it could be three hours . . .

Once when he was busy upstairs, and seemed to be taking his time doing whatever he was up to (not that I wanted to know), I decided to bypass trying to get his permission and just try phoning myself. I inched my way towards the fridge, but the precise moment I saw how I could reach it, I heard him start on his way back down. I turned as if I was about to go up myself. He didn't seem to notice anything wrong, but I felt myself pouring with sweat.

52

These days my mobile is my best friend. I keep all my messages, and I don't go anywhere without it. But when I think back to that other telephone, high up on its cold white pedestal, I nearly explode with fury.

Because that telephone was connected to the outside world with an ordinary outside line, just like anybody else's. I could have spoken to my parents. They could have known that I was alive and just waiting for them to come and get me out of there and take me home. At that moment, that's all I thought about. It would never have occurred to me to call the police. This monster was so sure of the hold he had over me, based on the fear that his story of the gangland boss had built up in me. I was convinced that my parents were as much at risk of being killed as I was. Knocked off, on the orders of the boss. He'd made that abundantly clear. And if I'd heard a strange voice on the other end of the phone, I'd have known it was one of the gang, and hung up straight away.

It was a huge risk, I knew. But the need to talk to my parents was overwhelming. He had persuaded me that there was no escape from him. Any attempt on my part would put my family in danger, but I'd had no news of them, apart from what he had told me, and the frustration was too much to bear.

I no longer know exactly what I wrote in my first letters home. Something along the lines that I knew what had happened must have been some kind of punishment, but that I'd had enough now. I asked about what had been happening, if they thought there was any chance of getting enough money to pay the ransom. I wrote about the creep – or rather, 'the man who was looking after me', as I diplomatically called him – and his 'paces'. I asked about what shifts my mother was doing at the hospital where she worked. I desperately needed reference points from the world beyond my own limited calendar. Such as the day we went to have lunch with my granny, my dog Sam's birthday, my mother's days off. Each night when I went to sleep I'd cross out another day, so that I wouldn't lose track of my life in this filthy hole.

Needless to say, I never got any reply to my letters, except what the creep chose to relay.

'Okay. Your parents got your letter, a friend of mine handed it to your mother. She said to make sure you eat properly, that you never were much good at washing yourself, and that you should enjoy the sex. And as they can't see how they can pay the ransom, you'll have to stay here. They're making the best of it, so you should do the same, now that you've got a new life and you're going to be my new girlfriend.'

I've forgotten now what other crap he invented to make me accept that I'd been dumped by my parents and left in the clutches of a monster with their blessing. Once – a good while later – he told me that they'd packed up all my things and put them in cardboard boxes, which was the equivalent of saying: 'You don't exist any longer. As far as your parents are concerned, you are dead. You will never see them again. And they don't give a shit about you.' It was unbelievably cruel. I imagined all my things – my old toys, my books, my clothes – in these boxes, in effect packing me off to oblivion. I no longer existed.

At the beginning I made out as if I was prepared to make the best of my new life, but I never really believed that my parents 'couldn't give a shit', as he put it, or had been glad to see the back of me. One day, they'd find the money and come and rescue me. I had told them what had happened, and how it wasn't my fault that I'd ended up incarcerated in this horrible cellar with this horrible man. And for all his machiavellian torment, it hadn't really worked, him telling me that I'd been abandoned – dead, as far as my parents were concerned. I stubbornly held on to the belief, or at least the hope, that it wasn't true. I just had to hold on. What else was there? Every day that I survived was an extra day of life.

I had been brainwashed, and the fantasy world that this creep had invented was so real to me that it fogged all sense of logic. Okay: I had been abandoned. But I still wanted to write to them, to explain that while I could accept my imprisonment, I had to admit that I thought it might have been as much their fault as mine. I had no idea what they – or at least my dad – could have done that warranted my being punished in this way, but I didn't want to blame them or make them feel guilty, because I felt guilty enough myself: for having let myself get abducted in the first place, then for having to endure this horrible man and the horrible things he did. At the same time,

I didn't know whether I could really trust them any more.

Perhaps the youngest child of a family always has the feeling that they don't really belong. Never doing anything as well as the others, feeling that they're somehow always in the way. So there was scope for this idea that I might just have been dumped. Even so, I was determined to survive, to redeem myself, to reclaim the love I felt I deserved. And I knew it was my fault because I hadn't listened to what I'd been told, hadn't thought enough about other people's feelings, hadn't cleared up when I'd been asked to. I'd generally been too selfish, too much of a loud-mouth. I'd never really been a very nice person at all, come to think of it. Now I was well and truly paying for it.

Sometimes I felt indignant that my parents hadn't made more of an effort to get me out. Even though during the first few weeks, I'd been convinced that my father would go knocking on every door in Belgium in order to find me. But once that first month was up, I'd thought, 'That's it. They won't bother to look any longer,' then 'They are looking for me, it's just that I don't know about it,' then 'They must think that I am dead.' I was in such a state of confusion, not knowing what to think about anything: about them, about me, about this creep. I was muddled and utterly lost.

Sometimes when he came to take me out of my dungeon, I felt – for a mad moment – as if I was free! Other times he just let me fester in my own misery. I never knew from one moment to the next what would happen. I would hear noises from upstairs, and I'd freeze, imagining that the gang, or even the boss himself, was above my head at this very moment. The irony was that after the terror of the unknown, the sound of his horrible voice saying, 'It's me' would come as a relief.

One day, when he was out, I decided to rootle around in the junk that was cluttering up the entrance to the hole, hoping to find something that I could play with that might help to pass the time. But it was just rubbish – a dead computer, cardboard boxes, broken bits of this and that. Nothing interesting at all.

I think it was then that I had first thought about writing to my parents. He'd said yes straight away. Of course he had. It wasn't as if he had any intention of doing anything with the letters, like posting them, for example. I think that in total I must have written five or six, though the investigating team that combed the place once it was over only found three: under the doormat. I wonder what he was planning to do with them – stick them in an album maybe? Or just have a good laugh at my misery.

According to my calendar, the second time I wrote was on 9 July. There's no trace of that letter now. I have no idea what he did with it, apart from read it, obviously. I never gave up hoping my parents would write back, that they would deliver me from this mouth of hell. But there was always this niggle in the back of my mind about the 'bad thing' my father had done to the boss. The creep had given me the impression that it was some unresolved thing to do with money.

Neither my incessant questions nor my tears resulted in anything other than more threats. Conversation, if you can call it that, was impossible. It was just variations on 'Shut up' or 'Stop snivelling'.

He would give me 'news' from home. I realise now that he could only have had one motive in letting me write the letters – and that was to turn the desperate questions of a distraught twelve-year-old to his own advantage. I had described, as well as I could, the things he had forced me to undergo. To which, my mother had 'replied' that I should be nice to him, and accept everything that happened without complaining, because if not, he would pass me on to someone else who would torture me. At twelve, this kind of instruction is beyond comprehension. How could I like the things he did to me? I was instinctively revolted by his actions – so how could I accept them?

There was also this idea that my parents had abandoned me. That they had their reasons for washing their hands of me, in short, that I was paying for something my father had done. It was a deal. By giving me up they didn't need to pay the three-million ransom. This brainwashing continued to work right up to the end.

I began to keep my eyes open for anything that might give me more of a hint of where I might actually be. In the Calvary bedroom, I tried to see between the curtains. I knew there was a railway track, and the little I had seen of the outside world was not in the least appealing. I was certainly not in Brussels.

The front door key began to exert a particular fascination on me, as he had taken to regularly leaving it in the lock. It's irritating at the best of times to be shut in somewhere and not to know what it's like outside, and I had a near-desperate desire to see beyond the front door, however dangerous it might be. Where exactly were the houses of the other members of the gang? And the boss's? Behind us? All around? And those trains: where were they on their way to? Where had they come from?

Showing me his gun was as much about impressing me as reinforcing the hopelessness of my situation. He kept it in a laundry basket on top of the kitchen wall units in the front room, opposite the front door, which must have been at least nine feet above the ground, so there was no chance I could reach it by myself. Since my father had been a policeman, I had some vague idea of what was involved.

'That gun,' I asked, 'what's it for?'

'For when I get weirdos coming to the door.'

He referred vaguely to 'one of the gang' I had never seen, not even a vague shape, let alone his face. If I was ever on the ground floor when the bell went, he would shut me in the second room before going to see who it was. And as the shutters in the next room were also closed, I couldn't see or hear anything. Nor did I try to. My instructions were to stay absolutely still and not make a sound. Everything to do with the immediate locality was controlled by the boss, and being spotted there carried a death sentence. I even convinced myself that the gun was there to protect me. Another little tweak of the scenario that I'd been made to swallow.

Down in the cellar claustrophobia had become a real problem. The appalling yellow of the walls made me feel positively sick, the foam of the mattress was disintegrating into dust. I was either too cold or too hot. I also had toothache. I had only complained about this once, because he had replied: 'If your teeth hurt I'll pull them out myself.'

My teeth, like my height, were about two years behind my age. I still had some of my baby ones, in fact. A few had been taken out, but there were still four adult teeth still to come. My toothache was agony. I just chewed on the alphabet biscuits, hard little things, that mashed up my gums. And as for a toothbrush, I could use it only when he took me upstairs. So whenever he was away on a 'mission' I couldn't brush them at all. It was the same with my knickers: I could only wash them upstairs, in the bathroom. If I used the water from the jerrycan in the hell-hole, it meant I didn't have enough to drink. It was the same when it came to washing my face. I had nothing. No flannel, no soap, no towel. Occasionally I'd put a bit of my drinking water in my mug so that I could at least wipe my face, and I'd then dry myself on the sheet on top of the disgusting mattress. I knew I was getting dirtier and dirtier. And as for washing me, he scrubbed me so hard that my skin would blister and I'd come out of the bathroom covered in red sores.

I could always daydream about our bath at home. Of the

little square of soap that smelt so delicious, and the softest, cleanest towel in the world. Sometimes I wondered what my parents would think if they saw me in this state. If they knew what it meant to have to endure this shaming scouring at the hands of this brutal excuse for a man who never made any attempt to actually get me clean.

The worst thing, during my jailer's absences, was the chamber pot. The smell was indescribable. I couldn't empty it until he got back. So, if he was gone for six days, it stayed there for six days, within inches of my nose. I could only scream and shout in my head. I couldn't even bang on the walls because, when he wasn't there, it was even more imperative to stay absolutely quiet. At any time another member of the gang might turn up, or even the boss himself. 'And if they were to hear you . . .' In reality I would have had to scream my lungs out for anyone to hear anything. The door to the staircase that led to the cellar was always bolted. But I was so terrified about the possible repercussions, that this order to remain silent was ingrained in me right up until the end. Exactly, I imagine, like the poor little girls who had gone before.

I was always trying to think of new ways to pass the time and to forget just for a bit that he would soon be coming to get me for the next session of 'his paces'. One day I decided to have another go at looking through the rubbish that cluttered up the space between the gate and the false door, if only because he had told me not to. I was fed up with copying out sentences, fed up with the stupid game, fed up with everything, fed up with him most of all. I also wanted to get back at him in my own small way. 'So, you don't want me to look through your miserable things? Well that's exactly what I'm going to do.'

I took it all very slowly, careful to leave no hint of what I'd been up to. There were bits of old computers. Dozens of cardboard boxes that I didn't bother with – they were piled right up to the ceiling and if I had taken hold of one, the whole lot would have come crashing down on my head. It was difficult to move in this cramped space, because the sliding mechanism for the massive door stuck out. But there was plenty to choose from, like shoe boxes full of papers. I didn't go through them that systematically because I was too scared of him bursting in at any moment. The first thing that I came across was some sort of document card, which I could never have guessed might be connected with my abduction. It was in the name of Michèle Martin. His partner, the mother of his two children, but – above all – his accomplice. Though obviously I had no idea at the time. But also I found three photos of naked girls. Poor quality, because they'd been taken from a very low angle. As I looked more closely, however, something went click in my head.

It was me, in the famous room with the bunk beds. The expression on my face was one of sheer terror. My eyes were swollen from crying and my body was covered with red splodges. The photo must have been taken when I was still suffering the side effects of the drugs I'd been given, whether on the first day or the second, I no longer know.

I wanted to tear them up. But then I stopped myself. What if he came looking for them and they weren't there? There would be reprisals, of that I was certain. I could just put them somewhere less obvious. As long as I knew where they were I could always destroy them later, if I ever got out of this hell. I felt so sad. It was pitiable to see myself like this.

Unrecognisable.

In the same shoe box there were more papers, keys and key-rings. But no more photos. The keys were of no use to me down here, and I would have recognised the front door key – I'd spent long enough staring at it.

So I had to accept that there was nothing else there but junk, certainly nothing that was about to improve my lifestyle in this rat trap. I was just standing up, when I noticed an odd-looking little box up on the support rail for the sliding concrete door. The rails formed a 'U' and the little box was stuck into the bend. I managed to prise it out. Even though it was covered in filth, I could see that in fact it was new – and filled with bullets. He wasn't exactly short of them. They must be for the gun I'd seen upstairs. I put the little box back in its hiding place. At least while the bullets were down here, he wouldn't be able to use his gun. Which was of course ridiculous, as he would certainly have had a supply in one of the rooms at the top of the house.

Later I learnt that the police found another gun in the hell-hole. If I'd only found it myself, and the box of bullets had matched . . . But would I have had the courage? Bang! Would that have been the end of it?

I had just put everything back when I heard his voice, with the weird accent that really grated on me: 'It's me . . .' The ritual greeting as he began to attack the shelves, taking everything off before raising the door to let me out.

Up there, in the Calvary bedroom, I could hear trains grumbling past, not far away. It drove me mad. Before, when I used to sleep at my grandmother's house, I would hear trains too, and it used to bug me because the noise would stop me sleeping. But then I'd put my granny's downy little pillow on top of my head, it muffled the noise and everything was all right again. Here it was far worse; I had the feeling that every train was thundering across the roof of the house, and they were never-ending. I didn't count them. I couldn't even see them through the window, but I heard them go by, perhaps ten or fifteen times a day, until I could hardly bear it. It was the one plus of the hidy-hole, as the concrete deadened the worst of the noise. Up in the Calvary room, the racket was dreadful.

Perhaps it's why I still hate trains, even though I never think of that room now. It may be unconscious, yet I am always aware of them, even when they're a long way away and other people can hear nothing at all. Unfortunately with my current job I have no option but to commute by train, shuttling back and forth between Tournai and Brussels twice a day, and I hate it. I just hope I don't die in a train crash. The idea that I might breathe my last knowing I'd been killed by a train would really get up my nose.

Ever since I'd first got there I had kept my eyes peeled. When I was down in the hole, I buried myself in my school books. I wrote, I drew, but I knew I had to ration my reading. I didn't want to use it all up. I listened to music, but that was a double-edged sword since all too often it reminded me of the life I'd left behind, and I'd break down in tears. Sometimes I did nothing other than ask myself questions to try to fathom the central conundrum: *He says he's my saviour, but all he does is be nasty to me.* It was beginning to drive me loopy, and the hell-hole itself would have sent anybody mad. I didn't even have a mirror I could talk to. I was always frightened of losing control. I needed things to hold on to. When he took me upstairs, and I could see that there was daylight, I would always note down the time when I got back. A cross on a date on my calendar meant another day gone, even if he hadn't come to get me. I would move my pot, and squat on the mattress to write. The pathetic plank beside the bed wasn't strong enough to lean on. I would change position, turn right round, but the walls were always there. So I decided to 'count my blessings', as he put it. When he had finished 'his paces' and had no further use for me, he would let me watch television for two hours.

And that was okay, even if he was always splayed out there beside me, the great oaf. The programme might be complete rubbish, but at least it was the world, reminding me that real life was still going on out there. Sometimes he would give me a yoghurt or three sweets, and I had so little to eat that even though I had paid for it by some obligatory nastiness – and this was not at all comfortable to admit – I'd devour the little pot with relish. I zapped from my mind the dirty things I'd had to endure by saying, *Go on. Eat your yoghurt, crunch your sweets, watch the telly*!

I could cope with all this. But any change to the routine, and I became totally disorientated and destabilised. One day, for example, he put me on the left of the table, rather than the right, which I found disturbing beyond all rational explanation. The first day that he told me we'd be eating in the second room, I freaked out.

'Why? What's happened?'

He couldn't have cared less – he had his own reference points, the bastard. Like his life. He could go cruising around in his disgusting little van taking in great gulps of fresh air, while I had to breathe in my own putrid air in that stinking little pit.

By now the hidy-hole was well and truly infested with brown creeping things that made sporadic attempts at flying. I hated squashing them, but I hated them being there even more. I have always had a horror of insects of any sort. I was covered with red blotches and I was always scratching. Was it only psychological? Or had they really bitten me? I don't know. At first, there were only one or two. So I got them with my shoe. But then they took their vengeance, multiply-

ing and multiplying until the place was teeming. My jailer
came and sprayed everything with insecticide so for two days
I had to sleep upstairs with him.

One day I found a drawing pin, or something sharp
anyway. Usually I wear studs in my ears, but on the 28th of
May we'd had swimming at school, so I hadn't put them in. I
told him that I wanted to use this drawing pin to keep the
holes open, but he refused to let me use it. So when I found
a paper clip I decided I would use that and just push it in each
ear, each day, then carefully stash it away on my little shelf. It
was pathetic really, how I tried to keep my space nice and as
tidy as it would have been at home. Especially since this pig
lived in a dustbin and his house was filthy. He treated me like
an animal and kept me in a hole even dirtier than the rest of
the place. But I needed my little routines just to keep myself
together, logic being in short supply in this lunatic asylum I
found myself in.

He drank coffee, but I wasn't allowed to, so I went on at
him until he gave me a little percolator. I was cold, so I went
on at him till he gave me some sort of heating. I pestered and
badgered whenever I thought I could get away with it. I don't
know how I carried on. From his perspective I must have been
a tough nut. Once he called me a 'bloody pain in the arse' –
probably when I was 'snivelling' too much. When it dawned
on me that he actually seemed to enjoy it when I cried, I
decided then and there to give it up, at least in front of him.
And in the end it was me who went and just got the yoghurt,

or the sweets, or the fruit if he didn't volunteer. I was not prepared to accept that I would be allowed to have something extra to eat one day, and not the next. I struggled against him as best I could, becoming increasingly aggressive and trying to put to the back of my mind his constant threats. But the black angel of Death was always hovering above me, among the filth and the tears.

After three weeks, or perhaps a month, I asked if I could do some washing. This was the moment he decided to do some washing himself. Not my clothes, but me. So that was another misery to add to the list. In two and a half months I wore the same pair of knickers, rinsing them out whenever I could in the bathroom basin, knowing only too well that they would take two days to dry. But they were the only ones I had. At the end of the first week, I knew that I smelled. I demanded that he give me back my clothes, but he told me to take a running jump.

Eventually he royally granted me the use of a pair of shorts and a vest, which were certainly not mine. What was going on? He'd taken them out of the huge wardrobe stuffed full of clothes, women's and children's. There were even some teddies in the agony room, and downstairs a cot. So why had he told me he didn't have a wife or children? In fact, he was always going on about me being his new 'wife'. None of it made any sense at all.

In French there are two ways of calling someone 'you'. There's what you say in families and between friends: 'Tu'.

And there's the formal way: 'Vous'. I always used 'Vous' with him. Not only to keep my distance, but I thought that if I was polite towards him, he might be polite towards me. Fat chance.

He was a liar. I continued to think of him as a total creep, with the stupid half-finished fireplace he was so proud of, and yet he thought I was half-witted. Naturally he considered himself a real brainbox, while really he was as thick as two short planks. If he actually had any children, well, I defied them to live with him.

Another 'mission' coming up. Goodbye to meals upstairs, to rancid mince. Goodbye to the agony room, peace for a couple of days. Hello to the Nic-Nac alphabet biscuits, the smelly pot, tinned food that dogs wouldn't have eaten. I'd write it on the calendar: 'Gone'. When he'd return I'd write 'Back'.

I hadn't been on my own for very long when suddenly, without any warning, the whole place was plunged into darkness. Pitch dark. No lights, no ventilator, no heating. Alone in this tomb, I was overcome by panic. I tried screwing the bulbs in tighter, then unscrewing them. The switch didn't work. I couldn't hear the ventilator. It was obviously a power cut. I would suffocate. I was already suffocating with panic. He had told me never to make any noise down here, as anybody could get in the house and hear me. But at that point I didn't care, and I began to scream and scream and scream, in the hope that he was still upstairs. Nothing. Nothing. So I screamed again: 'I'm in the dark! I'm not feeling well, the air is running out!' Nothing. I screamed again, my throat nearly bursting. 'The electricity's off. The electricity's off. Get me out of here!'

But nobody came. Slowly I began to calm myself down and, thank goodness, it wasn't long before the electricity came back on again. Otherwise I think I should have gone mad. Yet it had one positive effect. I was back in fighting mode.

'I'm getting out of here.'

I could see how to do it, in principle, but I didn't know if I had the strength. If I pushed against the bottom of the concrete door, putting my feet against the side wall to get my whole body weight (68 lbs) behind it, I might be able to get the sliding mechanism going. To my astonishment it seemed to work. I managed to get it to open by about an inch. But I was exhausted, and I needed to rest just to breathe. I didn't have enough leverage. The boxes shifted when I pushed them with my feet. I needed something more stable.

I drank some water before my next try. In the same position, I began straining again to try and budge this half-ton of concrete. And then suddenly there was the most terrible crash and the whole thing seemed to break up. There were two rails with runners on them and a metal bar that acted as a counterweight. And it was the bar that had fallen down. There was no way I could lift it, I simply wasn't strong enough.

For five minutes I'd been full of hope. Now it was worse than ever. I could neither open the door any further than it was already, or close it. And there was no way I could get through. An inch. That was all I had managed to achieve. On the outside there was a switch. But it needed a lever to make it work, and I couldn't reach it from the inside. There was only concrete. I couldn't put it back again, couldn't even pretend that it was nothing to do with me. So I just went back into my back bit, back to the yellow walls, to my mattress, and tried to read one of my books, to look like a good little girl for once, who would never dream of being naughty. I tried to come up with a reason as to why I might have tried to shift the door. I tried to psych myself up for whatever punishment he might devise, whose violence could only be guessed at. *He will kill me*, I thought.

Suddenly I heard a noise on the staircase. I remember thinking, *So that's it. He will just blow my head off.* I hid myself under the blanket, as I always did, waiting for the words, 'It's me.'

Nothing. Normally he'd be the one to open the door, and I'd come and I'd crawl out from under the blanket, reassured by the presence of my 'guardian-saviour'. Not this time.

'You stupid bloody idiot! What the hell did you think you were playing at? What would have happened if the boss had happened to be here? Do I have to spell it out? Well, if you'd left the house he would have killed you. Killing people means nothing to him. Nothing. And before he killed you, he'd have done things you couldn't even imagine!' I was expecting to be punished in some physical way. Hit or beaten. But he just kept yelling these threats, which went right over my head. All sado-masochistic tortures. To someone of my age they meant nothing beyond general horrors.

He never hit me. Not once. It was enough for him to lift his hand as if to go for me, and I could see the violence in his eyes and face all red with anger, the veins on his neck standing out like rope. And that was enough to shut me up, or get me to do what he wanted. His strength was not in his hands or fists. He repaired the door, and I never tried the same trick again. Psychologically, I was no match for him. What twelve-year-old would have been?

Rather than buoying me up, this failed attempt at escape had pulled me further and further down. I felt utterly helpless and powerless. I realised just how stupid I had been. Even if I had been able to open the concrete door, even if I could have broken through the one at the top of the stairs, even if I could have somehow got out of the house – what then? I'd have found myself in the middle of gangland, to be carted off to the boss, who'd hand me over to his torturer before killing me with a bullet in the head. I wasn't lacking in imagination, oh no, I had enough appalling details in my head to have it all planned out, right down to the final scene. And that was without even considering what might happen to my parents.

Guilt is as effective a weapon as any gun.

When I think that this monster only really wanted one thing: to satisfy his wretched desires on defenceless children and have them entirely at his mercy! He already had a whole raft of rapes to his credit, for which he had been arrested, tried, sentenced and imprisoned. He wasn't going to let that happen again. I came as close to death as is probably possible, while still able to tell the tale. And this feeling will be with me for ever.

Not once did I consider killing myself. Suicide never even entered my mind. Even if it had, I'd never have found the means. Luckily for me – and without even knowing it – I was a survivor. Hope was always there, tucked away somewhere, though I never gave it a name. It was neither tangible nor logical. It was a bit on the thin side. Puny, even. But in that day-to-day hell, it was always there. In my incessant demands for improvements in the level of comfort in my cell, I told him one day how – at home – I always slept with a teddy bear. So he gave me one, a forlorn old teddy whose original fur was so worn, it was hard to tell whether it resembled a bear or a dog. As far as the owner of the house was concerned, he was simply pathetic.

One day I will get out of this hell. I clung to this instinct night and day. And I needed to, as things were not about to get better in the days to come.

CHAPTER 4

Dear Mum, Dad, Grandma, Stephanie, Sophie,
Sebastien, Sam, Tifi and all the family,

    I've asked the man who is looking after me if I could
write to you because it's your birthday, Mum, and
yours, Sophie, and Sam's isn't that far away either. I am
very, very sad that I can't be there to wish you all a
happy birthday in person, so I could smother you with
kisses and maybe even presents!! What I thought I'd give
you, Mum, was an enormous bunch of freesias with a
few roses, or some flowers from the garden. For Sophie,
I thought of a Parker pen – if I had enough money that
is – and perhaps one for Mum as well, because I know
she'd like it too. And for you, Sam, a little toy, or a box

74

of dog biscuits, though I'd need money for that too.

JUST TO BE WITH YOU ALL – that's my biggest wish. But it doesn't look as if that's possible. Because the thing is, if I did come back to the house then we'd ALL end up getting killed, and I wouldn't want that!! I'd rather be here and just writing than at home and dead. I hope that you can read my writing and you're pleased to get the letter, because everything I've said here is completely true. I love you and I think of you all the time and it makes me cry because I know that you will never see me again. I hope that you think of me too.

I wonder if, when you eat something that you know I like, or hear a song that I used to prance around to, it makes you think of me a bit. I wonder if, when you've got music on, you still dance and sing and wiggle and waddle around like we used to. All I hope is that you're enjoying yourselves, and that you're eating properly (in any case it can't be worse than here!). And that you can think of me without it making you ill. Here the food is sometimes OK, but it can also be yuk. There's never any gravy to speak of, and what there is could do with a bit more flavour, though I hardly ever get it anyway. Mostly it's mince and tomato sauce, but all that does is give me stomach-ache.

I sent you a letter, which the man who's looking after me gave to a friend to hand over to you in person at the clinic. He told me, Mum – and all of you – that this

*friend had to take it there so he'd be sure to see you
alone, and nobody else would see him handing it over to
you, and that you had read it straight away and that
you'd said I wasn't to make myself ill by always looking
at the clock or my watch, and to eat well and wash
myself well. And that you also told this friend of the man
who's looking after me that I wasn't that good at washing
myself and also that you were all well and that you'd
come to terms with not ever seeing me again and that I
should 'enjoy' the 'sex' and the other things that I wrote
to you about in the letter. And that I should be nice to
the man who's looking after me because he could always
hand me over to another member of the gang and that
this person would finish me off, but only after he'd made
me suffer. He told me as well that Sam was OK and that
you are looking after my bit of garden and Tifi. Talking
of which, have you eaten all the radishes? If you wanted
to you could plant the rest of the seeds – there are still
some left in the packet, some of the red and white ones. I
think you'll find it in the shoe box with Dockers written
on the side, on the grey shelf in my bedroom – and I
think there are still a few flower seeds left as well. And if
they're not there, then you could try looking in the box
of sweets under the grey shelf in the cellar. It was you,
Mum, who said I should hide them somewhere, and
although I did tell you where I'd put them, I don't know
if you'll have remembered.*

When you have a nice supper, or a pudding, or biscuits or sweets, or anything else that you know I like, then think of me. Because when I get treats, it's only because I've done what he wanted – if you know what I mean. And when we get out of the bath, you should see the water. It's filthy and as for his hands, they're like coal. I know that he works, but even so. And then it's me who gets to clean out the bath. And it's worse than it might be because he always leaves the water in the bath to use in the toilet. He says it's to save on water used for flushing! Sometimes I even have to clean his disgusting toilet – because downstairs I've got my own chamber pot and when I go up to empty it into his, I always rinse it out properly – and the basin, and the floor, and that's all for the moment. I wonder what the weather's like outside, because there's only one window that I'm allowed to see daylight through and it's high up, more of a roof light, really. All the other windows have either got shutters or thick curtains that are always closed. And I'm not allowed to go outside to run about or play.

Are you going to be putting up the pool if the weather's nice? I'd so love to be there, with you and my friends. And that's another thing. This other man, the friend of the one who's looking after me, he says he doesn't want to hand over the letters personally any more. He says that it's too much of a risk. So you'll get them by post from now on, and the man who's looking

after me will give you a ring later, but I don't know
when or where. He might ask me for Grandma's phone
number, or someone else's, but I really don't know that
much about it. But there is another really big
problem . . .

The next part of my letter describes the various
things I was obliged to undergo and which I prefer
not to go into.

And that's not all: because he makes me sleep
without a night-dress or anything, he has seen that I've
got warts. Needless to say, he's decided he's got to do
something about them. So he's told me that he's going to
treat them with sulphuric acid. Of course I told him that
we've already tried all sorts of things. Anyway, one day
he came back with these bottles of sulphuric acid. And
then he got a match which he'd sharpened to a point and
then he began. When he saw how big they were, he said
that obviously they'd never been touched. So I pretended
that Dad had already done the same thing himself. Then
this morning, because it was two weeks since the last
time, he had another go. Normally when I feel it begin to
burn, then I have to tell him so that he'll stop, though
sometimes he carries on anyway. Yesterday (Saturday)
when I had a bath – I mean when WE had OUR bath! –
he scratched my skin with his hand until I was covered in

weals and looked completely red. 'I' have a bath once a week (1x) and when my hair is dirty, I get to wash it! The trouble is that the only shampoo he has isn't for greasy hair. The bathroom itself is filthy, especially the floor, and also there is no kind of mat. There's not even a door – it's just a curtain, and that's in shreds. There isn't even any central heating in this 'house'. I'm really sorry that I probably won't see you ever again. I'm sorry that I'll never be at home again. I miss our lovely warm bathroom, so nice and clean. And I miss my lovely warm bedroom, and my cosy duvet, a nice pillow, nice cushions and teddies and all my other bits and pieces. I miss good food like steak, chips, salad – chicken curry, rice – chicken with rice, white sauce etc. I wonder if someone could keep an eye on the shed for me. Has the mirror that was there been put back? The reason I told you about the warts and the infection was that if he asks you on the telephone how you did it, and you don't say anything, he'll realise I wasn't telling the truth and he'll take it out on me. Over the past few days he's really got to me, but I've had no choice other than to do what he wants. Sometimes I'm allowed to watch television but [. . .]

I have decided here not to go into the details.

[. . .] so you see that it's not exactly fun. And then, if it's getting near midnight, there's usually nothing much on.

Once I got to see the end of ER, the episode where Dr
Ross saves this kid by helicopter. I wish I could see Dr
Quinn or even Melrose Place. I haven't been very well
recently, it's like I've got this iron rod in my head, and
my nose is completely blocked up and the back of my
neck aches, and also my eyes. He's given me some cough
mixture and some nose drops. The nose drops are called
Nebacetine. I'm not sure if it's still all right, or even if
it's the right stuff for what's wrong with me. Also, all I
get to drink is UHT milk from cartons and tap water.
Sometimes – upstairs – I'm allowed to have a mug of
cocoa or a cup of coffee and sometimes a sweet.
Practically everything he gives me is past its sell-by date.
Then he just says that the date on the box is nothing to
do with the date when he got it! Once, when he was due
to go off for five days on one of his 'missions', he gave
me chocolate that was dated 1993! It did taste a bit
mouldy, but I ate it anyway. Most of the time he gives
me own-brand stuff. I haven't told him that we never
have anything but proper makes, but . . . Even the toilet
paper he gives me (when he does) is cheap and nasty.
Meanwhile he's drinking Coke (Yes, Coca Cola, The
Real Thing!) and Nutella, etc.

My clothes smell so awful that he's taken them away
to get them washed. So he's given me a little summer top
to wear, with short sleeves, but it's too tight, and some
bikini bottoms. And Mum, if you do get to speak to him

on the telephone, could you tell him the best way to wash
(if he's not washed it already) the red jumper that
Grandma gave me so that it isn't spoiled? (There doesn't
seem to be a washing machine here, or a tumble drier.)
Mum, each time you go to Gran's, could you give her a
big kiss from me (lots of kisses in fact) and before you go
to bed, could you kiss Sam's ears, in fact kiss him all
over? And for everyone else, imagine that I was giving
you a kiss every morning and every night and even at
other times. I would like to cover you all with kisses, and
wish you all the happiness in the world, and that every
wish you have ever had would come true. And last but
not least, Happy Birthday to Mum and Sophie.

You can't imagine how often I look at my alarm
clock and I tell you what I am doing or what I should be
doing, and I tell you not to give up, even if you aren't
actually working, and send you thousands and
thousands of kisses and tell you I love you and that I
want everything to be the best for you and my biggest
wish of all is to see you again, very very very soon, and
to hug you and never let you go. I gather that you've
packed up my things.

But was it all true, the things you said at the clinic?
You could tell me lots of things on the telephone just so
that I could have news of you, as I'm not allowed either
photos or letters. Have you found the photo album I
made of Sam? I meant to give it to you on Mother's Day

81

but I hid it so carefully that I completely forgot, so sorry. I hope that you'll like it. I SO LOOK FORWARD to hearing from you. !!! PS When he calls you, could you tell the man how you make your beer [sic] stew? PS And you could tell him on the phone what Dad got for Father's Day, and Sam too! PS I hope you like these drawings, but take no notice of my writing or spelling mistakes.

NB You might like to know that, when I've done enough reading, or am getting bored with the Sega, I sometimes get down to some school work! Oh, and I also forgot to tell you that some time in August there's a chance that another girl will be coming to join me, so we may get a bigger hiding place with its own bath and basin, etc. In the meantime, in this one I've got Nic-Nacs, bread, margarine (no butter), cottage cheese with garlic (not as good as the sort we get) and tinned food (not that great).

Also I forgot to tell you that when he treats the warts like I told you, he says, 'I'm a doctor and I know more about these things than your mother does.' (He knows that you're a nurse.) 'I know nearly everything, and how to do everything.' (He also hardly ever went to school.) But what's he going to do about my teeth? What if I need a filling? Or if I get something wrong with my eyes or my stomach or any other part of my body?

I love you all

I send you a thousand million kisses
FOR EVER AND ALWAYS

*And the man who's looking after me also told me that
he knew all about Dad having got into trouble with the boss
when he was in the police, something about Dad wanting
to borrow some money from him, and then hadn't given it
back, which is why the boss chose me to get back at you!
(or perhaps it was because of something else).*

*I'd really like you to hand over this money to put
everything 'straight'. Perhaps you should ask Gaetan's
granny, but it's probably too much because they'll want
even more now that he thinks I'm already dead, so he's
sure to want more!!! Oh yes, how did everyone take it –
the family and at school – when they found out?*

Tell the man what days you work and what hours.

*Also, the toilet paper here is like the kind you have
at the clinic, thin and rough so each time I go to the toilet
my fingers go through it – so not nice at all. And also,
sometimes, when the boss or some others come and stay,
he doesn't come to get me, so I can go several days
without having anything proper to eat! I hope I'll be able
to write to you again and, if I can't manage it for a
while, then I wish all of you the most brilliant time
possible (birthdays etc.).*

And I hope that you think of me!
My love to you all,
Sabine

*Have a really really good time during the summer
holidays, and tell the man whether you're going to be
working or taking time off and, if so, when till!*

It would take me several days to write one letter. I would wait until I had lots of things to tell them about. This one was dated 14 July, and I wrote 'letter' opposite the date on my calendar. I wrote 'left' opposite Tuesday 16 July and until 23 July, which meant that the monster was on one of his 'missions' and that I was alone in my cell.

Throughout my letters the sense is there that I had brought it on myself. Not so much that they didn't want to pay the ransom, but all the rest. I had written 'if I come back, I will be less selfish', but in fact I don't think that I had been that selfish. Now, I am, because I have to be, it's what I need, but I think I was over-worried about them because I was locked up, and so I said to myself, 'Perhaps I was too this, too that . . . so I should be less this, less that.' I thought I was being punished for all those things that my parents had told me off about. Not working hard enough at school, not helping enough around the house . . . So it was as if I was saying, 'I will be more obedient, I will be nicer.' But in the following letter I turned it the other way round, writing, 'So if I was such a horrible person, how come I did this or that?' which shows that I was attempting to temper this sense of guilt I was feeling, to the point where I was contradicting myself without knowing it. But it was the extension of the idea that never left me alone: *I am being punished. But what for, exactly?*

84

I may not have been everyone's favourite person, but I was a perfectly nice little girl. As I had lots of friends, I was out quite a lot, but when you're twelve you don't expect to be the maid, particularly with two older sisters in the house. I was still at the age when I needed to play, not vacuum, dust or do the dishes. Yes, I could be naughty, but my sisters had their moments as well. So over and over I'd find myself asking just how normal was it to be punished for such misdemeanours and, more to the point, in such an extreme manner?

I wrote, I drew, I watched the alarm clock, I carried on writing a letter I hadn't finished, I began writing poems for Grandma and the rest of the family, copied out grids for crosswords for my sister, wrote out a list of 'solecisms and barbarisms' from a dictionary, and even gave them advice on how to eat well and grow strong. I worked as hard at my writing as if I was getting ready for an exam. But even so, I was always inserting extra loose-leaf pages and, looking at them later, I found that my writing, the means of expressing myself, had changed. I had become at one and the same time more anxious, yet less childlike.

'As I'm not likely to come home – unless there's some miracle – Dad should have my radio alarm, and you should take some things too . . .'

'Even if I never come back, please, never throw away any of my things (please keep them) . . . think about me . . . when you are eating sweets.'

*

That Tuesday, 23 July, I had marked my calendar with a red star, which meant: 'Very, very bad'. Having come back from his latest 'mission', he had come to get me in my cell . . . Hours later, once I'd crawled back into my makeshift tomb – and barely able to move or think – I got paper and a pen and began, once again, to write. But this letter was addressed solely to my mother, and I could not contemplate reproducing it here word-for-word. Indeed my mother has never even read it herself. When the police found it – under the bastard's mattress – she had wanted to, but I've always said No. My suffering was enough. There was no need for her to take any of it on herself.

I wrote this letter of hallucinatory terror in the depths of my black hole, after such agonies as only my memory can bear witness to. I know that even this pathetic obsessive never had the 'pleasure' of reading it, as it was found in its envelope, stuck down, intact. It was the investigating judge who opened it.

I had accepted and indeed wished that my letters would be admitted into court and heard. They were read out in public by an investigator, to save me having to do so myself. My parents weren't there to hear them. I didn't want them to be put through it, and on the advice of my lawyers, they agreed.

The reason I decided to allow this letter to be seen by the jury and also – at least in parts – in this book, is that I want the truth to be known. Only then can people truly understand just how far a sadist will go in his obsessive desire for domination, in manipulating the psychology of a twelve-year-old child. The jurors were able to see it. Yet this man gave the impression of being intelligent. To the degree that he was a calculating, manipulative, and plausible liar, I could conceive it to be true. But for the rest – and I hope I will be forgiven this descent into the extremes of vulgarity – he was a scumbag, disgusting and utterly repellent, in mind and body.

The fact that I survived, and that this sickhead kept at least some of my letters, including the one addressed to my mother, shows just how stupid he was. These letters have served to prevent investigators and juries being gulled – by fantasies about paedophile rings – into believing he was no more than 'an intermediary', a 'poor victim' himself, which was exactly what he wanted everyone to think. Getting a girl of twelve to believe in the existence of a boss and a gang while she is locked up in a cellar in the most atrocious conditions, in fear of her life, is one thing. Convincing adults was altogether too ambitious, even for a self-blinded monster like him. The only people I saw were him and his sidekick-nerd in the hat, who was just as pathetic.

But this monstrous man continues to deny the truth about most of the crimes for which he has been sentenced to life imprisonment. This monster believed he could continue to play cat and mouse with the parents and families of his other young victims, just as he had done with the children themselves. And it's as much in their name as mine that I have wanted my letters put on public record.

I was his prey. His, and his alone. I was there to satisfy his sexual urges, and I am utterly convinced that once he had destroyed me and rendered me 'unusable' for his purposes, my fate would have been no different from that of the poor young girls and children who went before me: I would be dead. Had he not been caught, he would have continued blithely down his ruthless path, just like other psychopaths before him and to come, their wives trotting complicitly behind them.

He told me 'before': 'We're going to do it, to get it out of the way.' He told me 'afterwards': 'Stop screaming, it doesn't hurt that much. All girls do it. It only hurts the first time.' Finally he said that he'd 'leave me alone for a month'. But he did it anyway, and in a manner that was just as hateful to the young girl I was then.

I am not going to dwell on the sordid details of my physical state after this experience. Fortunately I eventually got over them. I have given only the gist of the first part of the long letter that set out the horrors I tried to forget, for a second time, after the trial.

Tuesday 23 July

Mum
The reason I have put on the front of the letter 'little letter just for Mum to read' is that I want to talk to you privately about some REALLY BIG PROBLEMS!
[. . .]

And then he brought me back down here into the hidy-hole. And now, Mum, I'm writing to you and I hope that you will have a good think about all this, because I'm going to ask you something very serious and very hard! If you only knew what he said to me and what I had to go through! He told me that I had to 'make love' with him and that it wouldn't hurt [. . .] that I had to kiss him, and you know how – he already made me kiss him on his mouth (vomit, vomit . . .).

I know I've asked several times already but you MUST get me out of here. At the beginning, I could put up with it, but now it's gone too far, and I'm really really unhappy. Once I had the following idea: I asked him whether, if you found the money (I know, money again), it would be possible for me to go back home. And guess what he said . . . YES.

Of course, there's a problem. As the boss thinks that I'm dead, even more money is needed (one million). So if you could get three million (as quickly as possible, please) and if I keep writing and he keeps telephoning, once you got the money you could let him know and then he could sort it out with you. Once he's got the money he told me he would speak to the boss and then I'd be able to go back home. Please don't think that I want to hurt you by asking you to do this, it's just so that:

1) I can see you all again, healthy and well if possible

2) I don't have to go through any more of this agony and misery but be happy again

3) we can all get out of this horrible business and go back to loving each other, even more than we did before.

I beg you, it's really very important for me and my life and the future. You know, Mum, I've been doing a lot of thinking and I hate having to ask you to do something like this, but please, please think about it. I just hope that you can win the jackpot in the lottery or even that television game show for families! I'm sure you could arrange it so that everyone could get their share. You know, I've really thought a lot about all that and when I was in the bed with the chain (before being rescued)*, I thought how in a day or not very long anyway, I'd be seeing you again! And I also thought about my life before, happy memories, but also remembered how naughty I had sometimes been, all the times I'd been horrible to you and not deserved to be loved. And I said to myself that the reason I was still alive was that God had given me a second chance to become a better person, in how I behave, what I say and what I do, and so I've made lots of NEW LIFE resolutions. Instead of always going out with my friends, I'm going to go over to Grandma's house, and rather than just hanging around the house in the

* This was the moment when he announced himself as my 'saviour'.

*afternoons when there is no one else there, I will pop
round to see her, and I'll spend more time with my
family and also more time on my HOMEWORK! You
know, I've looked at that school report several times
since I came here, and I can see now that I was worse
than useless.*

1. *because I didn't work hard enough.*
2. *because I hadn't thought how nice it would be for
   you if I'd had a good report covered with stars and*
3. *because (unfortunately) I never listened to you and
   just wanted to play.*

*So I've made up my mind to try really hard and to
do as well as Stephanie, which I'm sure Sophie will do
anyway. And there's something I'd like to ask you,
Mum: when you're at home, could we go through my
homework together, like we did when I was at primary
school? I think it's a good way to remember and not to
make silly mistakes like with 'Ambiorix'.* You
remember how we laughed about that! And most
important, the big things that I promise are (and it's
true) to be less selfish – for example, letting Stephanie go
on the sofa and also lending my things, being more
helpful, being better tempered, and lots of other
things . . . I'm sure that you will find that I've changed,*

---

* Ambiorix was a Belgian prince famous for defeating Julius Caesar in battle
in 54 BC.

hardly surprising after all I've gone through, but with your help and your love my broken heart will soon be mended . . . Please, please think long and hard about what I've said, but not too long. I can't carry on like this for much longer.

I love you,
Sabine

*Another thing, Mum, who's going to look after me when I'm ill, when my eyes are bad, or my teeth or my warts or other things? It's you who should look after me and teach me how to behave. I promise to do as I'm told.

*I probably haven't shown you enough how much I love you, all of you, but I do. And I promise to take Sam out for his walks more often.

CHAPTER 5

The 77th Day

Between this letter and the last one found by the police, dated 8 August, my health got worse and worse. I was haemorrhaging dangerously and in unimaginable pain. It didn't matter which way I lay, on my side, on my back, on my stomach – nothing made any difference, it was all the same. The only way I didn't turn was towards him, as I had not been returned to my cell but remained chained up in the Calvary room. All I could do to retaliate was to pull on the chain from time to time as the bastard snored beside me, brooding, *If only I'd had a knife . . .*

He had generously presented me with some Pampers, but which hardly helped at all as they were so thick and old that they needed to be changed every half hour. Back in the hell-hole, on that disgusting mattress with the blanket that scratched and between the suffocating walls, I cried. The worst thing was having no one to talk to about it. All I could hope was that the letter I'd written to my mother would get there quickly, and that she'd understand that I just couldn't take any more of this. The sense of my total abandonment had left me feeling both depressed and aggressive. Although I didn't see myself as a freak, I didn't recognise myself either. The girl on my school photo card had nothing in common with the person I knew I looked like now. I was filled with self-loathing.

The attack on my virginity, the violence perpetrated on my pre-pubescent body, and the refusal of this appalling, monstrous man to leave me alone – as he had mendaciously promised – made me want to kill him.

From time to time I would say, 'That's enough!'

He might reply or he might not. When he did, he'd say, 'It's not that bad.'

'But it *is* that bad.'

It was like talking to a toad. So I would just return to my inner voice, to talking to no one but myself: *He couldn't care less about what's happening to me. My blood could just drain away until there was none left, until I just died, screaming with pain, and even that wouldn't stop him . . .*

'Stop yelling!' he'd hiss when I just couldn't take any more. 'If the boss should hear you—'

Once I thought about saying, 'What if I counted up to a hundred, wouldn't that be enough?' And I began quickly to catch up: one, two, three, four . . . as quickly as possible . . . a hundred!

Like hide and seek.

Finally, for several days he did leave me alone, having successfully rendered me unusable for his needs.

I was really afraid that I would die. I tried hard not to imagine just how and when it would happen, but from time to time I would think to myself, *If one day this man kills me, I hope that he does it with a bullet in my head, so that at least it'll be quick.*

But I couldn't stop the images flooding my brain with the alternatives, given substance by his dreadful taunts of what would happen 'If the boss had any idea that you were alive', complete with details involving machines, ropes and belts.

I no longer recognised the face that looked back at me from the bathroom mirror: the bloodshot eyes; the stringy, dirty hair, the tracks of my tears striping my dust-covered cheeks. Among other amusements, he had wanted to cut my fringe, which was hanging over my eyes. The result was hideous. I drew a picture of what I looked like: my head as round as the moon, looking just like a clown, the fringe chopped off so short that it stuck out. As a contrast I did one showing my ideal: 'Hair cut by Dad or Mum.' The original I captioned simply 'Hair cut by him.'

I managed to retrieve a few strands to send in my next letter, neatly folded up in a separate sheet of paper. My fringe had been getting on his nerves for quite a while and he was always on at me to get it cut. I had even asked my mother – on a separate piece of paper – if that would be all right with her.

I had produced a kind of standard form where questions could be ringed YES or NO. Needless to say, it would be returned to me duly filled in.

Did you find the photograph album that I put together about my dog? YES
The little book of poems? YES
Birthday presents? YES
Boxes (meaning what my mother had packed away)?
No reply to this one.
Teddies or other soft toys – if they have been packed?
No reply to this one.
Am I allowed to laugh? YES
Drawings – what did you think about them?

He had attempted some kind of reply, but it was clearly his writing and not my mother's:

'There quite nice' when it should have been 'they're quite nice', a mistake my mother would never make – and there was nothing else about what the pictures might have meant to her. Anyway, nice wasn't her kind of word. *Anything else?* And in the same handwriting he'd written what he wanted to do. 'Cut fringe.' I was sure now that this hadn't come from my mother – and particularly since I'd now seen the writing. In fact, I'd been suspicious ever since he'd reported that my mother had said I should 'wash better'. My mother would never have said anything vaguely like that. She knew that I was perfectly capable of washing myself and, anyway, this bastard's version of personal hygiene was in no way related to keeping clean. And the haircut stuff didn't hang together either. My mother wasn't that bothered about what my hair looked like – she made fun of it, really. If she'd said anything at all it would have been, 'Do what you like.'

Perhaps he suspected I was becoming suspicious of where the information on the forms was coming from, because from then on these kinds of detail arrived 'by telephone', so there could be no question of my querying the handwriting. Strange though it must seem, although I was beginning to have my doubts about specific details, I still believed totally in the sick scenario of the boss and his underworld gang.

'Your parents have given up looking for you. They haven't handed over the money, so they must think that you're dead.'

'But they can't!'

While I could accept that they had given up searching for me – they were doubtless afraid, being in mortal danger themselves – as for thinking I was dead, that I could never believe. I believed they'd got my letters, so why should they think I was dead when they knew where I was? Through my jailer's machiavellian cunning I was being dragged deeper and deeper into despair, doubting even the natural bond between a daughter and her parents, the fault line being my mother, whom I'd always suspected of not really wanting me around.

I was the baby of the family, so when she would joke that my arrival had been 'an accident', I would translate this as her wishing I'd never been born, and say to myself, *I'm just a waste of space*. When I refused to do the sweeping or the washing-up, I was 'nothing but a pest'. And sometimes, when she'd go on about how one of my sisters was Little Miss Perfect, I'd cast myself as her polar opposite, the Stroppy Little Madam, good for nothing – except, that is, failing maths.

So from my vulnerable twelve-year-old perspective, my abandonment had seemed perfectly logical: 'Good riddance to bad rubbish.'

One more torture to add to the list.

The cogs in my head were turning overtime, trying to balance the desperate see-saw of hope and despair. One moment I'd be up: *It's not possible. Stop thinking like that!* The next I'd be wiped out again. *It must be true: all this time, and I'm still here.* Then back up again: *But they know I'm not dead because he's talked to them on the phone!*

I had got to the point where I was running out of ways of resisting him, as I had made it a matter of honour to do right from the beginning. But because I'd been kept in such a humiliating and increasingly debilitating physical state, it became more and more difficult to say No and devise ways of getting my own back, though when he was sleeping I'd have little bursts of creative energy.

If I could just get hold of that gun he showed me, and get it to work, I'd kill him stone dead!

Fat chance – I was chained up.

Often when we were eating and I had my fork in my hand, I'd be thinking: *I'd like to jab this right in the middle of your fat face!* I became obsessed with that fork and what I might do with it. But where should I aim for?

Locked up, lonely, with only this arsehole and his schedule of horrors for company, I began to crack up. I did nothing. Nothing interested me any more. I was fed up with writing. I didn't even know what to write about. As for the Sega console, I thought I'd broken it one day when I'd gone a bit berserk. In fact I hadn't, but I couldn't bear to watch any more of those stupid graphics. I had read all my books, and rereading got me down. I turned over the pages without taking in a word. And those last weeks I felt increasingly lonely, as he locked me up in the rat-hole and disappeared on yet another of his 'missions'. I had nothing to cling on to. I talked to myself, I looked at the walls, I stared at the ceiling – as if by some feat of imagination I could pass through it.

My imagination was not limited to my own private fantasy, however. It was hard at work on practical solutions – as I saw them – to secure my release.

'Set me free!' I promised him. 'No one will say anything to the boss, and if necessary I'll go and live somewhere miles away. So what you could do is warn my parents that we'll have to move house, and then we'll go burgling and break in somewhere – "pull a job" – to get the money.'

There was nothing I wouldn't have done to get out. At

first I had simply detested this man, but now it was reduced to pure hatred. How dare he leave me here, locked up, without even any fresh air to breathe. Without being able to go upstairs to eat, even though I knew what would be in store for me on the floor above. The air wasn't that much better up there, but at least it was different. Which is more than could be said for the scintillating dialogue that accompanied our meals – always the same.

'This muck is disgusting.'

'Stop whining and just get it down you.'

'I want to see my parents.'

'Not possible.'

'I don't want to go upstairs. I don't like it.'

'Tough shit.'

For two and a half months, this lack of ordinary conversation had slowly driven me mad. Eventually I came up with an equally mad idea.

'I want a friend,' I said one day around the end of July.

'Not possible.'

But how else was I to survive this hell? I couldn't write any more, he wouldn't set me free, so I had to have someone to keep me company.

'I've got no one to talk to. I'm fed up. I've got masses of friends at home. So why can't I have one of them?'

'Because you can't, that's why.'

And from the expression on his face I could see he thought I'd totally lost it: *Oh, I see, just go and knock on a door*

*around the corner from you and ask if one of your friends wants to
come and play?* And of course he'd have been completely mad
to go anywhere near where my parents lived, into the district
where everyone was searching for me. A criminal never goes
back to the scene of the crime! But from my perspective, the
idea of getting one of my friends to join me was not unrea-
sonable. I mean, it wasn't as if I was asking him to open the
door and let me walk free. I didn't let up, and – as was usually
the way – I was soon in tears.

'Don't you understand,' I whined. 'I'm not used to being
shut up like this. In summer I'm always outside, in my little
shed, or in the pool! With my friends!'

So then he came up with the idea that I should 'sunbathe', and he made me lie out on two chairs shoved
together – naked, naturally – underneath this see-through
corrugated bubble-stuff that passed for a roof-light. It would
give me the feeling of being in the sun, he said. I told him
there was no point taking all my clothes off because everyone
knew you couldn't get a tan through a window. But still I had
to do it. Five or six times we went through this rigmarole. It
was uncomfortable and completely ridiculous.

I still clung on to the idea of a friend. When I think about
it today, I console myself with the knowledge that, by this
stage, I was cracking up. It seems to me now that I had
regressed to being a five-year-old. My rant went something
like this: 'I'm bored, I'm fed up, I don't like being alone, if you
don't want to let me go, then at least let me have a friend!' I

was acting like a spoilt child demanding this and that until its parents eventually capitulate. I had no idea that he had ever kidnapped any other children. I thought I was the only one this had ever happened to and that in fact he had 'rescued' me from a hideous fate. So why couldn't he just bring one of my friends to visit me? Someone who'd just come and play for a bit, even stay the night so we could sleep together? I didn't imagine for one second that this friend would be forced to suffer what I had gone through. I was the hostage. I was the one whose father had done this bad thing to the boss, so there'd be no reason to punish my friend. But – as he kept reminding me – it just wasn't going to happen.

On Thursday 8 August I had written my last letter to my parents down in the hole. Even if they had abandoned me, even if they did think I was dead, I didn't care; I had to write to them. But my loyalty was buckling under the pressure. I felt they weren't doing enough to help me get out of this place – they were just leaving me to rot in misery. Not that these feelings are directly expressed in the letter, but between the lines there is a poignant undercurrent of bitterness.

Dear Mum, Dad, Grandma, Stephanie, Sophie, Sebastien, Sam, Tifi and all the family,

I was very pleased to hear all your news. I know that he wasn't able to talk to you on the phone for very long because he didn't want to make a nuisance of himself. I haven't got as much to say in this letter because it wasn't that long ago that I wrote to you the last time. I was also glad to hear that Sophie's godfather had been to see you, she would have liked that. And I hear too that Stephanie passed her exams, and I'm very pleased for her and I'd like to congratulate her because she deserves it, and Sophie too, even though she didn't need to pass anything to get into the sixth year.

I wonder what present Sophie's godfather gave her. And you too, Mum, and Sam. And perhaps, if you've got the time, Mum, you could tell the man what you got. I know you've put up the pool and that you're taking advantage of the fine weather. I hope that the holidays will be really sunny and that everyone has a brilliant time. You also said, Mum, that I should look after the infection. But you obviously don't realise that he's really hurt me very badly and he has completely broken my hymen and made me bleed. It's true that he's been kind enough to let me write to you, what with all the risks he's already taken for me. But you know, life here isn't all fun and games. The house is a disgusting tip. As for the bathroom, well you don't want to hear about it. (No bath mat for a start.) You know Mum, I know that you said you were cured from that time you were really ill, but it frightened me when you said, 'If it comes back again, I'm not going to do anything about it', I love you so much. I'm happy too that Sam and Tifi are all right, and I hope that my radishes were good, and

that the flowers are doing well. I am 'happy' that Sophie
has taken Myositis and Marsu*. In any case, I had
already told her that if anything ever happened to me she
could have them. I know too that Dad has got my radio
alarm and that he had to change the batteries. To change
the time of the alarm you have to open up the back.

I'm pleased as well that you have all forgiven me
and wish me luck. I hope that Gran is well and that her
arthritis won't come back. I hope too that Sophie was
pleased that I went in to see her when she was in the
clinic for her operation, and that I wasn't too much of a
nuisance. Perhaps she'd have preferred to have been left
on her own to get a bit more rest. You know that even
though sometimes we argue and get on each other's
nerves, it doesn't really mean anything. We like each
other really. If I honestly didn't love Sophie and
Stephanie, then I wouldn't have been interested in
whether Stephanie had passed her exams or not, and I
wouldn't have bothered going to the clinic after school to
see how Sophie was getting on. And if I didn't love Dad,
then why would I fetch his jumper from upstairs or his
beer from the shop, or his packet of tobacco from José?
And if I didn't love Gran, why would I have helped her
to bring up milk and things from the cellar? or got the
coffee tray for her, or helped her hang out the washing
and carry the basket back in when it started to rain? And

* Two of my soft toys.

*if I didn't love you, Mum, why would I run off to fetch
a bottle of oil or vinegar or whatever from the cellar?
Why would I go to the bakery for you? and iron
handkerchiefs and other things, or take towels or the
basket, or other stuff upstairs? And why would I give
your feet a massage in between your toes when you're
tired, or when we used to go to bed early, at the same
time? Why would I do all these things for you all if I
didn't love you? You might have come to terms with not
ever seeing me again, but what about me? Have you
thought about me? After all, I never did anything to this
'boss', and so I don't really see why I should be the one
to suffer. I'm really sorry to have to say things like this,
especially after everything that you've done for me, but
you really must try and do something to get me out of
here. I'm really very unhappy and I miss you so, so
much. It's true. For one, I want to come back home
because I want to see you all again. For two, I would
like to come back home because I don't belong here, I
belong with you, with the whole family and with my
friends, and also because I can't stay a moment longer in
this dump. And for three, he hurts me so much—
[. . .]
And also because I don't want to grow up here, because
when you're twelve to thirteen it's when everything's
about to start and the last thing I want is to get my
period here. Because these disposable nappies that he*

105

gives me break up in just a few minutes. (And they're just own-brand things, so not exactly comfortable.) In an earlier letter I told you that I had bread, but it's not like proper bread we get from De Roo's or Maes, it's sliced factory bread in a packet, made by machines, or something like that. And it isn't even butter that I get, it's margarine! I told you as well how he was going off on one of his 'missions', and it happened! He was away between 16 July and 23 July. But when he came back it was bad news for me. Anyway. Then he was away between 1 August and 8 August. And on 8 August he went away again till? (I don't know when he'll be back, because that's today, 8 August.) Anyway, all I hope is that you're all well and that you're enjoying the summer holidays though that doesn't stop me always looking at the clock and crying when I think of you. I love all of you very much

Sabine

PS On the separate pieces of paper I've included some crosswords for Sophie, and some poems I've written all by myself without any help! Also some drawings and a list of solecisms and barbarisms I copied out of a dictionary that he 'gave' me. (He is really a nothing sort of person, and can hardly string more than two words together.) The hair that's in the folded up piece of paper is mine, but it wasn't me who cut it – he did.

He's made me look like a clown, far worse even than when Mum cut it that time. You'll get the idea when you see the picture I've drawn. (The grid – for the crossword – isn't as good as the ones Sophie does, but I did my best.)

He is sure to give you a ring within the next three weeks or so.

NB He says that I can call him 'Tu' but I prefer to keep my distance!! I forgot to tell you that when he goes off on a 'mission', I'm allowed a little coffee percolator so that I can heat up water (it's Nescafé – not as good as what we have at home, but better than nothing!)

As he was leaving, he told me, 'I'm going to bring you back a friend.'

I didn't believe him any more than if he'd said, You can open the door and go back home. I had reached a point where I could see no end to it all, and believed that I would stay locked up in this hole for at least ten years. My parents obviously couldn't have cared less about the things I'd described. I could suffer the torments of the devil, but nothing was going to change.

He got back that same evening, 8 August. I marked this date with another sad cross on my calendar. On the 9th I didn't see him. He is marked as 'left'. On 10 August he came down to get me from the hell-hole. I thought it was to bring me up to have something to eat. But no.

'Your friend's here,' he suddenly said as we went up the stairs. 'You'll see her later.'

I was staggered! And happy, because I knew I'd been going a bit mad and so having someone else around, apart from horrible him, seemed like a miracle. Obviously I wanted to see her straight away.

'First a sun-bathing session, and then you can see her.' This stupid performance irritated me at the best of times, but now it was worse than usual. When he eventually took me upstairs, I quickly grabbed hold of my bikini bottoms and put them on, not wanting to appear totally naked in front of my friend. And I remember feeling cross that I'd not had time to put on my top. After all I didn't want her to think she'd strayed into a mad house where girls wandered around stark naked.

And then I saw her, this other girl, this 'friend', chained to the bunk, and I could see that under the sheet she was as naked as I had been. I had this terrible sensation of having been here before.

She didn't look at all well. He tried to wake her up so she could see me.

'This is your friend,' he announced.

I didn't understand. She wasn't a friend of mine; I'd never seen her before.

'Who is she?' I asked. 'And what's her name?'

I realise now that he had no idea. Anyway, he didn't reply. And I had this strange feeling of being happy and anxious all at the same time. I didn't know where she'd come from, and as I still hadn't really worked out that I'd been kidnapped, rather than 'rescued', I had no reason to suspect that she'd been snatched from her family either. I just supposed that he must have gone to see someone he knew, and mentioned how he was looking for a friend for this girl who was getting bored with being on her own.

As I was looking at her, trying to adjust to this change in my fortunes, the reality began to dawn: the bunk bed, the chain around her neck . . . it was like ticking items from a checklist in the vague recesses of my memory, till – looking across at her, as if to check that there really was someone here – it hit me like a hammer blow.

Oh God, what had I done . . . what had I done . . .

She had opened her eyes and, as I stared at her, I saw myself: the sheet, the chain, the naked body underneath – it was me. And I wanted the earth to open up and swallow me. Instead I just said what I would have said anywhere, to anyone.

'Hello. All right?'

I didn't know what else to say. And with that animal right beside me, listening to every word . . .

'What's your name?' she managed in a muzzy kind of voice. She'd obviously been drugged.

'Sabine.'

'How long have you been here?'

I lowered my eyes, afraid of telling her in front of him because it would be like writing my own death warrant. I'd thought about it a lot. If he knew the exact number of days, it might be just the excuse he needed to decide that he'd had enough of me and that I was getting to be a drag, so time to get rid of me. And I knew that he could. Just like that.

So I said it as quietly as possible.

'Seventy-seven days.'

But she was already asleep. She'd been there since the night before, though of course I'd had no idea. I hadn't heard a thing.

CHAPTER 6

80 days

'Do you want me to wake her up?'

'No.'

He took me back down to my hole saying that he'd let her sleep. I was in shock, and frightened. First to meet someone for the first time chained to the bed just as I had been, and then to find myself back on my own again. My mind was racing. Where had she come from? I didn't want him to wake her; I was afraid of finding out that she'd been abducted like me, and if her parents paid the ransom and then she went back and told them she'd seen me, he'd kill me.

The next day, 11 August, he brought me upstairs for something to eat. There were three of us sitting at the table. I had hoped to be able to talk to her, but she wasn't much better than the previous day, and he was always there watching us with those sadistic black eyes. She refused to touch the food he'd heated up in the microwave. All she would eat was some bread and margarine while staring out into space. *She must be still drugged up to her eyeballs*, I thought.

I'd been feeling increasingly unnerved since the moment I'd seen her the night before, chained up to that bed, and thought, *Shit, it's a carbon copy of what happened to me*. And then the dawning realisation that I was the one who'd demanded a friend. I dreaded to think what he'd already done to her. Yet at the same time, there was a terrible kind of relief in knowing it wasn't me. And in knowing that at last I'd have someone else to talk to. But for that, I would have to wait until she got a bit better and he brought her down into the hidy-hole. Only then could we have a proper talk.

The dark future that I'd been expecting with only him for company was beginning to brighten. There was a patch of blue sky in my bleak despair. Now at least there would be two of us. And he had promised to make the hidy-hole bigger by clearing out the rubbish in the glory-hole bit. He'd even said he'd get a basin plumbed in!

In the meantime he put me to work cleaning the house. Armed with just a bucket, a dirty towel and some washing-up liquid, I had to clean the bathroom, the side room where we ate, and the front room. I'd done it all once before, but I don't remember when. There had been some kind of flood and there'd been mud everywhere and he had accused me of being a princess because I had complained at the state of the drying-up cloth. This animal didn't care about dirt: he was as filthy as his lair. He'd never allowed me to clean up the hidy-hole since I'd first got there, and it was now so mouldy and dusty that my nose was permanently blocked. Even so, I refused to let him get any drops for it.

While I was banished back to my rat-hole, he kept my new 'friend' upstairs. He'd tried to get her to walk around naked but she'd managed to get back her clothes and then he'd let her keep them on. The next day, Monday 12 August, I noted on my calendar 'Friend', which marked her arrival underground, and as the heavy door fell back against us, she looked around our dungeon through half-closed eyes.

Her name was Laetitia. I suggested first that we should have something to eat. She shook her head.

'No. I'm too scared that he'll drug me again.'

'You must eat something,' I said. 'You've had nothing since you got here.'

'Yes I have. Bread and butter, just none of those heated-up meals.'

I managed to get her to eat a few Nic-Nacs. The first thing I wanted to do was to warn her about the awful things he would try to do, probably the next time he came to get her. 'He already has,' she replied. She had experienced the same kind of 'induction' that I had. It was difficult to talk about. I didn't dare ask too many questions, though I did ask how she'd managed to cope. By gripping the bed, she said, and not crying out.

113

'I was too frightened he'd clout me.'

'But that's mad,' I said. 'He's never hit me and I've screamed my head off, yelling that it wasn't right and that I wanted him to stop, and that it hurt.'

'Well, you look like you've been beaten up,' she said. My eyes were swollen and bloodshot from so much crying, and my skin was still covered with red blotches, so in fact it probably did look as if I'd been punched and kicked.

'So, been here ages then have you?' she managed in her slurred voice. 'And you're okay?'

'Depends on what you mean . . .'

I passed her my calendar to show how I kept track of the days. It was extremely important for me, the only link I had with the world outside: who was doing this-or-that course, the days my mother had off, the day my grandmother came to visit, and also, of course, a parallel record of the days the animal left on his 'missions'. And the days he returned.

'I've been here since the 28th of May.'

She looked at me hard, peering as if she could only just make me out. He must have given her more drugs than he'd given me.

'Wait a minute,' she said slowly, 'what did you say your name was again?'

'Sabine.'

'Sabine what?'

'Sabine Dardenne.'

'I've seen you before.'

'Well, I've never seen you,' I said. 'Where do you come from?'

'Bertrix, right up by the border.'

'Well, I'm from Tournai, the other end of Belgium, so we can't know each other.'

'But yes! Yes!' Suddenly she seemed to wake up. 'I remember now. Your photo is everywhere, and that's where I've seen you. Belgium is covered with posters of you, and your parents are going mad trying to find you!'

'Well, they're not trying very hard,' I said. 'I mean, you've seen my calendar. Today is my seventy-ninth day here.'

'But of course they're looking for you. And I haven't made a mistake. Those posters are you – I just needed to make the adjustment between the photo and you here. And believe me, your parents are desperate to find you!'

I didn't believe her. My parents couldn't be looking for me because they were perfectly aware of the situation. And, anyway, they hadn't paid the ransom.

She asked me how I'd got there.

'I was on my way to school, and they snatched me off my bike. And you?'

'I was in Bertrix, and I'd gone to the swimming pool down the road with my sister and her boyfriend and some friends of mine. But because I had my period, I didn't actually go swimming. My sister and her boyfriend went off somewhere so I hung around for a bit, until I got fed up with watching everyone else having such a great time, and decided to go home.

115

The pool isn't that far from our house, so I walked back. And then this old van pulled up and the driver asked if there was anything going on in Bertrix. I told him it was the twenty-four-hour Scooter-thon. The bloke made out as if he didn't quite understand, and in less than two minutes, I was bundled up and that was that.'

'Was it the side door? By him?'

She nodded. While the nerd with the hat, who'd asked the question, had started up the engine, the bastard had come up behind her and grabbed her. After that, it was exactly the same story as mine, except that they'd wrapped her in the blanket to bring her into the house. Laetitia was two years older than me and she'd been too tall to fold up into that box. We learnt later that the neighbours had in fact seen her being carried in, but he'd calmly told them that it was his poor son who'd been taken ill.

'He gave me some kind of pills,' she said. 'But I spat them out. Then he tried again, with some Coke. I spat them out again. Then he said, "So you think you're the clever one, eh?"'

What he hadn't noticed was that Laetitia had spat them straight back into the bottle. By the time he saw that the Coke was foaming, it was too late – he'd drunk the rest of it himself.

'The third time he shoved a whole lot down my throat, which is why I'm still so drugged up.'

She was speaking very slowly. Every so often I asked if she

116

wanted some bread and butter. And she'd say no, still half asleep.

'So what do you find to do down here all day long?' she asked eventually.

Although I'd been warned not to say a word about our way of life, he'd told me to explain how it all worked with the hidy-hole. How, at the slightest sign of noise, we had to get down here, and were only allowed to speak again when he said the words: 'It's me.' Then I gave her a tour of our domain. There were the two lamps, one weak and the other a bit stronger, so that you had to disconnect it to turn it off. Anyway, I explained, I kept it on all the time as I was frightened of the dark. Then there was the shelf, the chamber pot, the tins that only juice could be drunk from, the jerrycan of water, the bread that went mouldy overnight, the little percolator and the instant coffee that I got given from time to time, but no sugar. He didn't believe in sugar. I would get given three lumps and have to eke it out, rationing it to make it last.

Laetitia listened to me, still half asleep. And I so much wanted her to wake up so that we could have a proper talk. From the moment I knew I had a 'friend', all I wanted to do was talk. But it was obviously very hard for her to stay awake.

'You've got a telly then?' she said, looking up at the ancient box on one occasion when she came round.

I explained that it just acted as a screen for the Sega

console. 'If there was a telly at least I'd have heard some news, though I do know that we are still in Belgium.'

It's fair to say that this, our first day together, was disappointing for me since she was asleep half the time. The next day wasn't much better, and I often felt I was talking to myself. I showed her my satchel, which I'd been allowed to keep, and my lessons. I told her how I'd been writing to my parents. She asked whether I thought she'd be allowed to write home as well. I told her how it had been really difficult. 'Because it's all boring, and I just needed someone, so now you're here.'

She was so drugged up that it hadn't occurred to her to ask, 'You stupid imbecile, so I'm here because of you?' The story he'd told Laetitia was that this wicked boss of the underworld gang had it in for her, but – thanks to him – she'd been rescued just in time.

'He told me exactly the same thing,' I said. It still didn't click. Perhaps if Laetitia had been more awake she might have begun to see the connections. But she was out for the count.

We were like sardines on that mattress. I had tidied everything as best I could at the bottom of the 'bed', but it wasn't going to work. How were we both going to breathe in this rathole? I could barely breathe as it was, without someone else using up the air as well. Being locked up like this was torture for me. Even as a child, I had hated to be cooped up. I needed space, the freedom to kick a ball, just to run around outside. Here I would become like a mad dog. I probably was one already, I realised. Look at me: dirty, disgusting shorts, top black with grime.

And then, lying squashed up against this other girl, I had a thought. When I'd tried to get the concrete door open, I'd failed mainly because I didn't have enough strength, though there had been a moment when the gap had nearly been big enough for me to get my head through. So with two of us, we might do it! But even before I'd talked about it to Laetitia, this brainwave was abandoned. He'd nearly lost it when he'd found out the last time, and if the two of us tried and it went wrong again – who could say what he might decide to do. Although Laetitia was taller than me, I sensed she might not be as strong when it came to dealing with physical violence – which I was sure was how it would end. And even if we could manage to slip through the gap into the cellar, what then? There was still the door at the top of the stairs, which was always locked. There were also the two ground-floor rooms to get across to reach the front door, also locked. All this without having the faintest idea what lay in wait for us outside. After all, we were in the heart of gangland.

I tried again to get comfortable in this minuscule space that was now supposed to fit two of us. But it was hopeless. Laetitia was stretched out on the mattress, still not at all well, and I didn't really know how to squeeze myself in. It was worse than a sardine tin. She spoke to me once or twice during these two or three hours, while I felt increasingly stupid for having asked for a friend. It just hadn't occurred to me that he would try the same trick.

When he eventually came down into the cellar he told me to stay where I was. It was Laetitia he wanted. I could guess what he was planning to do with her, but in one little corner of my head, I felt relief, knowing that at least for a bit I'd be left alone. Later I was ashamed of even thinking like this. But I'd very nearly gone mad over the two previous weeks and suffered so very much. That barbarian didn't give a damn about me. I could be bleeding or screaming, yet he'd do whatever he felt like. And I knew my turn would come sooner or later, so I might as well try to make the best of this respite. When he'd said to me, 'You stay where you are,' I had nearly come out with a *'Phew!'* from sheer relief. It's sad, but that's how it was.

The day before, when he'd brought her down into the hole, he'd taken the opportunity to remove the little radio alarm, so now I couldn't even listen to my music. I did some singing anyway, but ended up crying and singing through the tears. I was terrified that my watch battery would give out, and I'd not be able to keep track of where I was. I thought about what Laetitia had said, how she'd just clenched her teeth together and clung to the side of the bed because she was frightened of being hit, and it worried me. If she didn't fight back, then he might get the idea that she was okay about it all. This bastard was so stupid, he might even believe it! But how could it be okay? This little turd was less than nothing, and I hated him. I just hoped that Laetitia had shown him how much he disgusted her.

When she came back, she said nothing. But I looked at her, I knew this wasn't the moment to talk about any of it. In fact, I didn't dare. Each of us would have to cope as best she could, I decided. Screaming, yelling – either way, nothing changes. And he was perfectly capable of hitting her: I remembered how I, too, had been terrified he'd do something like that to me, those times when he would bang his fist on the table and tell me to 'shut the fuck up'.

Laetitia began properly to emerge from her semiconscious state on the fifth day after her abduction. It was 14 August. She was hungry, and apart from some bread and butter and Nic-Nacs, she'd had nothing to eat since she'd arrived and was still afraid he'd drug her again, she was only just beginning to get over the first lot.

'Are we allowed to eat the stuff in those tins?' she asked.

'You can if you want to, but I warn you, it's crap.'

'I thought I might give the meatballs in tomato sauce a go.' She managed half of one of them, but eating cold, tinned food like that is disgusting.

'Couldn't we try heating it up using the percolator?' she suggested.

'How? We haven't a saucepan or anything we can use to cook with down here, so it's cold or nothing. The lot: the gravy and all the gunge. Bread goes green within two days. Only the Nic-Nacs are really edible. Otherwise it's just water or milk – assuming it hasn't gone off. If the carton is kept closed, it does last a bit longer.'

You couldn't hear a thing down there, not a footstep, nothing. Just silence.

Laetitia told me that he'd kidnapped her on 9 August, the day before the last time he'd forced himself on me. The monster was insatiable. He had made Laetitia take some contraceptive pills (past their sell-by date of course). Apparently he had a whole stock of them.

We'd been on our own now for more than a day. He must have gone off on a 'mission', I decided. Lucky for us. Except that we hadn't had the chance to ask for extra provisions, so we'd have to make do with what was left of the tinned stuff and the bread. We had nothing to wash ourselves with. But as we agreed, that side of things wasn't his strong point. He was utterly repugnant.

As the hours went by I began to find it rather odd that he hadn't come down to get us. He had his 'needs' and hardly a day went by without him annoying me. I had imagined that it would be the same with the new girl. And I said as much to Laetitia: 'It's all a bit weird.'

And weird it must have felt on the afternoon of 13 August, for our jailer to find himself on the wrong side of the bars. We knew nothing about it, obviously. The irony was that an officer of the child-protection squad had actually been to the house with a search warrant and had found nothing. We hadn't heard a squeak. Laetitia had been fast asleep and I should have been sleeping too, but in any case if we'd heard the slightest noise, we'd have frozen until we'd heard the words in the accent that could curdle blood:

'It's me.'

After it was all over, that poor officer was called every name under the sun. They gave him such a roasting at the trial, they had him in tears. He had done all that the search warrant permitted, including inspecting the cellar. And to be fair, I would defy anyone to discover the cunning mechanism of that concrete door – hidden behind the swing-out shelves filled with stuff – without the benefit of heat-seeking devices, or high-tech listening equipment. If the bastard had owned up straight away, then Laetitia would have suffered less, even though he'd done his worst on Day One. As for me, given the point I had reached, forty-eight hours more or less made little difference. Whatever. No way did I, or do I, reproach this poor man. He has no reason to feel guilty.

It was the afternoon of 15 August. I had already put a cross over the date. I'd done it before when he hadn't been down to annoy us, and it signified a day of truce in this every-day war against evil. I still had no sense that peace would ever come. One more day and I would have been there eighty days and the same number of nights, bar one.

From the time on my watch I knew that in the world out-side the sun was setting; inside we had only our Nic-Nacs to eat. Perhaps I showed Laetitia some of my drawings or my school work to pass the time; I don't remember any more. In order to sleep we had to squash up against each other on that disgusting mattress less than three feet wide. And that's how we were when suddenly there was a noise.

'Did you hear that?' I whispered.

'What?'

'It might be the boss and his gang.'

I didn't have to spell out what that meant. Laetitia knew as well as I did how we were dead meat if we got into his hands, and that this bastard was our only protection. She had swallowed the fairy tale just as I had. He was her saviour. I don't know how long she had believed it, but that's how it was now.

'We must hide ourselves under the blanket,' I said. 'If he says the words, then we can get out.'

We heard the faint sound of footsteps coming down the stairs and then alongside the shelves that ran the length of the secret place.

'There's too much noise,' I whispered. 'I've never heard so much. Something's not right.'

We could hear men's voices, calling out in every direction, but indistinct. Danger was inching closer and closer towards us. This time, there was no escaping it. We were utterly terrorised under that blanket, shaking with fear. As Laetitia was still under the influence of the drugs, she was if anything even more stressed than I was. She had less of a sense of what was going on, except the sure knowledge that her life was in danger. I was a bit more together and, not wanting to scare her even more than she was already, did my best to reassure her, even though I was absolutely terrified. As the 'veteran', I took it upon myself to judge the level of danger. I knew I had to think for both of us.

'Do you think it's him?' she whispered.

'Look,' I replied. 'I've been here two and a half months, so I've got more to lose than you have. Either they've come to get both of us – and in that case I don't know what will happen – or if it's just one of us they're after, then that's obviously me. They've come to kill me. We'll just have to wait.' I don't think there could have been a millimetre between our trembling bodies, so closely were we jammed against each other, face to face, so that we could whisper.

First, we heard the noise of the bricks being scraped across the cellar floor, and then the clank and hump of bottles being moved, and then the low thump of plastic containers being taken down from the shelves. Now I was truly afraid. Naked fear, the sort you can't hide, knowing that death was on its way.

'Laetitia,' I finally managed to whisper. 'There are a lot of them and I'm scared. I've never heard this before. They're moving the bottles now, so any minute they'll be in.'

And then we heard his voice, exactly as it always was.

'It's me. I'm coming in.'

The door slid heavily open, with just enough room for us to get out. Suddenly I was gripped with terror. It was him all right, standing on the little step where he always waited, but behind him and around him were many other men. I was filled with the most terrible panic, driven mad with fear.

'I'm not coming out,' I shouted. 'I don't want to come out. Who are all these people? You're going to kill us. We're not coming out.'

And to Laetitia: 'Look, I know it's him, but these men, we don't know who they are.'

But very quickly, Laetitia put her hand up, her finger pointing.

'Yes, I do. I know him! I know him!' I followed the line of her hand to the men crowding the cellar. 'He's from Bertrix. He's a policeman! Come on, Sabine. Don't be afraid. Just let's get out!'

At that moment, we were persuaded – both of us – that, true to his word, our 'saviour' had found a way of saving us, he'd gone and got the police. I hesitated for a second or two, stupefied. I turned towards him.

Was it true? Could we really leave? I even asked whether it would be all right to take the coloured pencils he'd been so 'kind' as to give me.

'Yes, you can have them. Yes, take them.'

Idiotically, I said, 'Thank you!' And, as we had to pass him to get out, like an imbecile I reached up to give him a kiss on the cheek. Laetitia did the same.

I find it nearly impossible, even now, to accept that I had believed it all, right up to the end. That this cretin, this man without a name, this piece of shit, had the nerve to come back. At the time – though everything was happening so quickly and I was trying to make sense of it – I just thought that he must have got bored with the situation and, not knowing how to get out of it, had called the police. As for that 'Thank you' – if only I'd had the wit to spit in his face. When I think how I missed this opportunity!

We flung ourselves into the arms of the first policeman it happened to be. I found myself clinging to Michel Dumoulin, and after the trial, many years later, he told me what had happened. 'You didn't want to let go, you were holding on to me so tight,' he said.

I hadn't remembered any of that. But as he spoke, it all came back to me like a horror film in slow motion, frame by frame. The two of us under the blanket, trembling with fear, the door sliding open, all these people, strangers – you could even call them a mob. And then everything on fast forward: I slid under the door and collapsed into the arms of the first policeman I saw, and I wouldn't let him go.

Laetitia fell into the arms of André Colin, the policeman she'd had the luck to recognise because he had lived nearby. He gave her his handkerchief, and she began to cry. As for me, I was seized with a delirious excitement: I would be leaving, at this instant! I was going to get out of this place! I couldn't have cared less about the rest of it. I suppose that the violence of emotion engendered by this liberation was the mirror of the fear I'd had only seconds before. It was all so sudden, to go from the life of a rat in a hole where I had stagnated for eighty days, up into the bright light of the summer sunshine. I was hyper!

I thought I would faint when I got outside. I hadn't breathed fresh air for so, so long. And I couldn't stop talking, as if I was a mad woman. 'I'm so happy! Tell me it's true. Is it true that I can go home? Are you sure? Am I going to see my parents? Am I going to see my mother?'

I was euphoric. I was no longer afraid, but trembling with relief, with sheer joy and excitement, and of course I cried. I think I must have been nearly hysterical without really realising it. This wasn't a joke, then? A dream? Was it really true?

The next thing I remember is being in the police car, clutching my pencils, headed in the direction of Charleroi police station, faster than I had ever been driven before. I must have left the pencils on the back seat of the car, or in the police station, because I never saw them again, though I remember clearly holding them in my hand. I was still dressed in that little pair of shorts and the disgusting top, my hair like a witch. But I was exultant! In the car one of the officers looked at me as if he couldn't believe I was there.

'The whole thing is unbelievable,' he said, completely stunned to see me there. It had been Laetitia they'd been looking for that afternoon. They had long since given up any hope of finding Sabine Dardenne alive.

So it was all thanks to Laetitia's having been kidnapped, and the swift police action that followed, that I was brought out alive. Because sooner or later, he'd have grown tired of me.

Lie as he might, this creature whom I wouldn't dignify with the name of Slug had developed a habit of kidnapping little girls or young women in pairs. I'm no detective, but the *modus operandi* was telling. The way he perpetrated his crimes was always the same. The evidence was there in his actions. Three times, at least: us, An and Eefje, Julie and Melissa.

I do not wish to shirk my responsibility for having asked for a friend. But I had asked for this friend with the innocence of a twelve-year-old, together with a certain madness and pig-headedness induced by the isolation he had kept me in. I believe now that the monster was simply preparing his reserve supply. When I had become 'unusable' Laetitia would surely have taken my place.

It may be that I succeeded in nudging him a little ahead of his schedule. But whether he had already planned something of the sort is now of no relevance. What is important is that the day Laetitia was kidnapped, his disgusting van was spotted. The first witness was a nun, who looked out of her window, irritated by the noise of the broken exhaust, which was on its last legs. (A metal worker – for that's what he was – should have known better – his negligence shows his crass stupidity.) Next he was spotted by a student, who described the crappy white van with its pronounced rattle, a Renault Traffic it turned out, plastered with stickers all over its windows. This boy had remembered the first three letters of the registration plate. And from that, the police had traced the owner of this heap of rust, a serial sex-maniac with a criminal record as long as your arm.

He had been taken completely by surprise and arrested in his own back garden. He was immediately handcuffed, in less time than it took him to drag me off my bike two and a half months earlier. His wife was by his side.

At police headquarters in Charleroi, I still hadn't heard the end of the story.

They asked if we wanted to see a doctor. I said No, what for? I wasn't ill. I was still hyper, but clear-headed. 'What I want is something to eat, something to drink, and I'd like to have a wash. I want to get out of these disgusting clothes. And to see my parents!' The officers continued to watch me warily, unnerved by how I was reacting. They confessed later that they'd been unable to grasp how I could have emerged so apparently unbowed. It was incredible for someone of my age, they said.

Perhaps. But then, I've always been impatient. All I wanted now was to get home as quickly as possible. My father had been told and was already on his way, they said, and he'd been asked to bring me some clean clothes. It would take an hour or so to get here, as we lived some way away. I couldn't do much about that, but nothing else mattered now.

I was over the moon with happiness.

CHAPTER 7

Welcome back

The vending machine at the police station didn't run to anything very interesting, so they just went for the most filling things they could find. I was deciding which to eat first – the chocolate biscuit or the honeycomb wafer – when one of the investigators came and sat down beside me.

'Sabine,' he began, 'I'd like to introduce you to the investigating judge.'

What was an investigating judge? I asked. The officer explained that he was in charge of gathering all the information before the case could come before the court, that's how the system works in Belgium. What case? Then I looked up at the man standing in front of me.

'Are you the investigating judge?' I asked.

'I am.'

I turned back to my policeman. 'But he's wearing a Hawaiian shirt!' I might not have known what an investigating judge was or what his job entailed, but any kind of judge was obviously someone serious, and while a tropical-style shirt might have been all right on a beach, it seemed totally out of place here. It strikes me now that he might well have been on holiday, because no one had expected to find me alive.

The people I met that first afternoon were as dumbfounded as if I'd popped out of a Jack-in-the-box.

I couldn't understand what the problem was. I still hadn't got my head around it. I had no idea that Belgium had been covered with posters of me and my bike. I hadn't even believed it when Laetitia had told me the same thing. It was all very confusing. I was free, that I knew. But how or why was beyond me. The scenario that I'd been spun by that bastard was still my central frame of reference. I don't know how Laetitia was taking it, but as we had both said 'thank you' to him, even gone as far as kissing him, I imagine it must have been much the same for both of us. So the first thing the police had to do was to put me straight about that aspect. Their explanation went roughly like this:

'Those stories of his were pure invention. He lied to you. He wasn't your saviour – quite the contrary.' They'd had their suspicions about him for some time, they said. He'd been in prison for things like this before and had a substantial criminal record. 'Sabine, you were conned.'

That short final phrase went into my head like a dart to

the bullseye. I knew it was true, and I suddenly saw the whole thing for the comic-book fantasy that it was. Once again, my reaction would surprise them.

'Did you say he was here?' I asked.

'In a cell down the corridor, yes.'

'Then take me to see him, because I've got a few things I want to say.'

'Now then Sabine, just calm down . . .'

Calm down?! How could they tell me to calm down? Didn't they see? I'd swallowed every single word he said, like a complete brain-dead idiot. I had even said 'Thank you'! That was the worst. If I could have rewound the tape, I'd have wiped that out. I was a pathetic imbecile.

By this time I was fuming, and if the police had let me get anywhere near him, I think I'd have beaten him to a pulp. I'd show them how to deal with this arsehole. *Thought you could fuck me over, did you? I'll see you rot in hell.* The explanation should have come as a relief, but it only served to unbalance me further. I was only twelve, but – as everyone knew – a stroppy little madam. And I was reacting as if someone at school had played a nasty trick. All I wanted was to insult that bastard sadist, and sort him out on my own!

It was a strange mixture of emotions, rage and euphoria all at the same time. I didn't know whether to laugh or cry. Yet while all this was going round and round in my head, I was also thinking about what I had to look forward to: seeing my house, my parents, going back to school. But where were my parents, shouldn't they have been here by now? And what were they going to say? What was I going to tell them? After all, I'd already told them pretty much everything in my letters. But perhaps they hadn't got them . . .

It's difficult all these years later to analyse just what was going through my mind in those first few hours of freedom. Guilt, shame at what I'd had to go through, anger, happiness at being free. Not that I made any kind of list, consciously or unconsciously. I dealt with all these contradictory emotions on pure instinct.

The police officers had all said that I had nothing to worry about, and not to ask too many questions. 'You'll be fine,' they said, 'once your father gets here.'

By now I was flying high.

'What about my mum?' I asked.

'Your father decided it would be better if she stayed at home. He needed to know first what kind of state you were in.'

'But you told me I was going to see my parents! And now you tell me I'm only going to see one of them because of my "state"? My state has got nothing to do with it! My mum would just be glad to see me.'

Yet again, they all thought I'd lost the plot, or was ill, and went on about how I should see a doctor. Even when my father eventually arrived, I had a good mind to have a go at him too for having left my mother behind – but of course, I didn't. I said only how everyone had been really nice to me, how I'd been given something to eat, and how everything was great, but that now we should get going, because I was a bit fed up. Then he started bombarding me with questions, and what with him, and me, and the police all trying to be heard, it was like a madhouse.

I don't remember feeling any emotion when my father came through the door. I certainly didn't burst into tears or fling myself into his arms. I just wanted to get out of that place. I'd had enough of it. I was free and that was all that mattered. He gave me the bag with my clothes in and I went with a welfare officer to the ladies' toilets, degrimed my face and got changed. Laetitia was doing the same. She had met up with both her parents. Normal life was about to be resumed.

Once I had emerged, I tugged on my father's arm. 'Come on Dad, that's it. Let's go.'

But by this time there'd been a call to say that my mother was on her way. A friend of hers from work was driving her down. She had decided she had to come, no matter what anyone said, and although I was really glad to see her when she did finally arrive, by that time I had reached saturation point. All I really wanted was to get out of that police station; I'd have run home if I could. And then it was my mother's turn to bombard me with questions: 'How are you? Are you feeling all right? We've been so worried . . . searching for you everywhere.'

'I didn't know you'd bothered. I was there all by myself. I hadn't heard a thing.'

I can't remember now exactly what she asked me. But it always seemed to end up: 'So you're okay then?' – 'Yes, I'm okay.' I was in one piece, that was the important thing. Perhaps I wasn't feeling one hundred per cent brilliant, but nothing called for an answer other than 'okay'.

As I stood there with all this going on, what I really felt like saying was, 'Come on, no more questions. Just leave me alone, at least for tonight, and let me go to sleep in my own bed.' Looking back, I suppose that after my release, everyone had been expecting to see a wreck, a traumatised little girl in floods of tears. But I'd done enough crying in that hole to last me a lifetime, and after living eighty days with the threat of death hanging over me every minute, there was nothing to frighten me now. Adults saw things differently. I was the victim of a serial sadist. And that was all they saw: child abuse. I didn't want to think about it any more. I had escaped from the jaws of death, and I was alive. No more fear, no more pain. My instinct was telling me: Get back to what you know – your bed, your teddies, your everyday life.

Mum, Dad and I set off for home in an unmarked police car driven by an officer from our local police squad. When we arrived at the Tournai exit, the famous bridge I'd cycled under that morning of 28 May on my way to school, I saw a huge banner: 'WELCOME'. People from our neighbourhood had had just enough time to get it made. It seemed the word had got around as if by magic. It took me completely by surprise. The road we lived on was full of people walking towards the house, and cars were everywhere. It was like a massive street party. I was already anxious and tense, and this unexpected homecoming was unnerving, to say the least. Our police car couldn't get through for all the crowds of people and journalists with their trucks and satellite dishes. I couldn't even see the red brick front of my house. I could feel a sense of panic welling up in my throat. I've never liked crowds at the best of times; I feel imprisoned by them. This mass expression of excitement was just as frightening.

'What's going on? Who are all these people?'

'You've been missing for eighty days, Sabine. It's only natural that people want to celebrate!'

I couldn't imagine how they all knew that I'd disappeared. But they were just some of the many thousands who'd been searching for me without let-up, scouring the countryside for clues, dredging the river. A special incident centre had been set up to look into the disappearance of the Belgian children, Julie and Melissa, eight years old. An and Eefje, seventeen and nineteen, me and Laetitia, and others. I knew nothing of the shock waves that would echo around the world at the news of the arrest of the Monster of Belgium. It was as if the whole country had been in a state of high tensile suspense, and at the arrest of 'the most hated man in Belgium', everything imploded. What followed would shake the country to its roots and ignite a whole series of political fires and resignations, from government to grass-root investigators. Even the judge in the Hawaiian shirt, and my real-safe saviour Michel

Dumoulin. Years later, I would find myself at the heart of a gigantic controversy, living witness to a cowardly and lying psychopath whose testimony would cover thousands of acres of newsprint and fill millions of people with panic.

I only knew what had happened to me and, to a limited degree, to Laetitia. That's still the case today. It took me a long time to assuage my own guilt in having asked for a 'friend'. It put me, I felt, in the same category as the monster, even though I knew with the rational part of my brain that it wasn't my fault. Though I had been stupid enough not to think that he might do the same thing all over again, it was he who traumatised her, not me. I had been so desperately lonely, incarcerated with this madman, that I had been numbed to any other considerations.

I told the investigating officers what I had done, and that I was the one who had asked for a friend. But they knew perfectly well that my brainwashing had been so complete that I should not consider myself in any way guilty. And they told me so. However, over the intervening years this guilt has always been with me. I've tried to rid myself of it by saying that if I hadn't pestered him for a friend, I would be dead now, because he wouldn't have been arrested. But I'll never be rid of it completely. Laetitia knows it. But I'm sure that even if she's never actually voiced it, she doesn't hold me to blame. We spoke about it, during the trial, and she knows I have enough of a burden to bear as it is, without needing anything extra. I was desperately unhappy about my unwitting role, but what it boils down to is that Laetitia saved both of us.

Back at home, I wasn't able to analyse things so clearly. It was only a few hours since I'd escaped from that rat-hole where the bastard had brainwashed me with his scenarios of ransom, death, parents who didn't give a damn. And suddenly I found myself in the midst of a crowd of people who'd been looking for me all this time. It was impossible for me to connect these two contrasting images. I had believed the bastard, and I felt angry with myself for being such a stupid idiot as to fall for his pathetic scenario. That was the one thing that really had got through to me by then. The one thing that dominated my thoughts.

A policeman lifted me over the rose bushes into our front garden. I said hello to lots of people without even knowing who they were. And when a microphone caught me saying 'I've missed you', it was picked up by the media and broadcast round the world. I hadn't said it to anyone in particular. It was general. I had missed my life.

When I got to my front door, I recognised my friends from down the road while one of my sisters took me straight into her arms from the policeman who'd carried me from the car. I could hear the crowd behind me, cheering and shouting, but suddenly I was oblivious because there, in the doorway, stood my grandmother. As she held me close, she whispered quietly in my ear, 'I am so happy to see you.' And at that the floodgates opened, as they hadn't done when I'd first seen my father. Grandma, my rock, whose love for me was unconditional.

The house was full to bursting, to the point that there wasn't even enough room to sit down on the sofa. So I found a space on the floor, next to the table in the sitting-room. I wanted to hear all that had been happening to everyone while I'd been away. I wished I could have had a remote, to zap from one person to another, but also to edit out anything to do with me, the one thing I didn't want to talk about. In fact, I have never told my family about what happened. If they read about it in the newspapers later, well, there was nothing I could do about that.

I went up to the bedroom I shared with my sister. I wanted to see my teddies. The vast crowd were still there outside the house, bonfires lit for burning the 'Sabine Missing' posters. I peered out from the bathroom window, lifting the curtain just a bit, but without turning on the light. I gave a little wave to the crowd and up came a sound of clapping as if their lives depended on it, echoing between the houses in my road.

On my own in the bathroom, I wept. It was completely mad, these strangers cheering and clapping like that when all they could see was the faint outline of a shadow. And it scared me.

It was quite a long time before I emerged from the bathroom and went to bed. But I felt good, something almost like happiness. The battle was over and now there was peace.

That's how it would stay, I decided. I opened my wardrobe and looked at my clothes. Checked that my cushions were all still there. Checked my parents' bedroom, and my other

140

sister's. In the sitting-room I'd noticed a few new things, a couple of lamps, and some cushions that they must have bought while I'd been away. And I remember feeling this strange resentment – though at twelve, I probably wouldn't have known the word – which I expressed as simple shock: 'My God! They bought all this new stuff while I was down in that rat-hole?'

The next day the headlines on every newspaper were the same: FINALLY FREE! ALIVE! There were pictures of both Laetitia and me, all the details about the massive hunt and how we'd come to be found. I felt deeply ashamed. To think I'd doubted my parents and chosen instead to believe the bastard and his sick stories. I felt unutterably stupid, humiliated to have fallen for his load of comic-book crap.

On 16 August there was a steady stream of visitors to the house, people coming with flowers and other presents. A firework display was put on in front of our house, organised by the estate. It was really nice of them and made me feel wanted, but at home my family were still asking, 'Are you okay?' and I reassured them, 'Yeah, I'm okay.'

On the morning of the 17th, the investigation team whose job it is to prepare the case (not something done by the police in Belgium) came to the house to take my statement. That same evening we saw on the news that the bodies of Julie and Melissa had been found, buried in the garden of a house in Sars-la-Buissière that belonged to the bastard. Those two poor little girls, only eight years old, had disappeared in June 1995.

The footage showed the mechanical digger and the holes in the garden. I looked at the screen and felt shock waves go through me. I had come to within an inch of the same fate. It could have been me in that garden. And Laetitia, in due course.

Those horrible pictures took me straight back and I could feel my courage begin to collapse. Yet, as if in response, I felt something in me harden; I was determined not to fall back into darkness. I knew instinctively that I would have to distance myself from it all, from the fear of death that had hung over me for over two months.

That morning I found it hard to talk to the investigators again. It was all too soon – I'd barely had time to draw breath. But I knew I had to, while my memory was still fresh, before I forgot anything. Occasionally their questions would get to me, and they would pull back. 'If you'd rather we stopped,' they said, 'we could take a break, and then carry on later. The last thing we want to do is upset you, but this is all very necessary. You must tell yourself that none of this was your fault.'

I knew that the bastard himself was being interrogated at the same time, and I was determined not to let him spin his ridiculous yarns a second time. I knew I had to tell everything that had happened, before I forgot even the smallest detail that might turn out to be crucial to the case. These were the men who had nabbed him, set Laetitia and me free from the grip of his monstrous claws, and I had utter confidence in them. I knew that I could and should speak to them. But to nobody else. I still didn't want to see a doctor, though in the end I had to. It was necessary for the investigation.

But that evening, seeing those pictures on the television, I knew I couldn't handle it. The next day all I wanted was to run away, at least to my friend next door. Or even pathetically to sit in my shed, just to enjoy the last few days of freedom before school went back. It wasn't easy – I had to tough it out with my mother just to go next door to my friend's house, barely three yards down the path.

For those first few days I was terrified of going out, even to see my friends. Terrified of strange looks and questions. But none of my fears were realised. My friends weren't stupid, even though they were only my age. To be honest, they had a better understanding of what I felt and needed than certain adults around me.

'Be careful, and whatever you do, don't go outside,' my mother would say.

'Okay, okay. But what do you think's going to happen? It's the middle of the day, the estate is full of people, the sun's shining. There's even someone mowing the grass. I want to go outside!'

I wasn't afraid of anything any more. I just wanted to go back to how things were before. People on the estate had clubbed together to give me a new bike, and I saw no reason why I shouldn't cycle to school. But the answer, of course, was No. 'Not on your own. Not yet.'

'Are you really saying that I can't ride to school because of what happened? I'd have to be really, really unlucky . . .'

It's true that, at the beginning, I was a bit wary. When I'd hear someone walking behind me, for instance, I'd look round just to see what they looked like. It might only be someone from the estate going to get a newspaper or a loaf of bread, someone I already knew by sight. But whoever it was, better to register their face, just in case.

Luckily I've always had an eye for detail, and I was able to describe everything about the abduction itself: the nerd in the hat, his jacket, and all about the house. Everything that I'd noticed or heard was etched on my brain. That's the kind of memory I have. Details stick. However, in every other respect, I've got the memory of a goldfish! Even before it happened, I'd always been able to remember things like car numbers and telephone numbers – it had been a bit like a game. But now it was real. If I saw anything vaguely resembling a camper van, I took to memorising the number plate, even if there was nothing dodgy-looking about it at all, even if it was just an ice-cream van.

So I did take a bit more notice of things around me, but only a bit. What I needed was to get my life back, my normal life, not a dose of paranoia. Nor was I about to start telling young girls about how they should live their lives. Warn them? About what? Of course, we always think that these things only happen to other people, and that's patently not true. But bad things can happen at any corner of any street at any time. Like the story of little Loubna – another of Belgium's missing children – who went to the shops on an errand, and who was jumped on at the petrol station at the corner of her street. Who could have foretold that some bastard was going to kidnap her at that particular garage, put her in the boot, and kill her, so that her body wouldn't be discovered till years later? Nobody. And there is nothing anyone can do to prevent it. There I was, cycling along on my way to school, minding my own business . . . Who could have foreseen what happened to me? Nobody.

I can't remember now the first time I rode back from school on my own. But I do remember that I wanted to as soon as possible. If my sister happened to ride alongside me, well, she used to do that before. I would set off on my own, but she'd soon catch up.

Back at home, though, it was over-protection city. My mother was the worst culprit, and I was not that sympathetic. Our neighbours were now equally paranoid, and their children were no longer allowed to go outside to play. I wanted none of it. I didn't want to talk about what had happened, and I particularly didn't want my mother to read the letters that I'd written down in the hell-hole, which had now been found by the police. 'But you wrote them to me in the first place,' she insisted. 'Surely I've got a perfect right to read them.' I refused, and to this day she still doesn't know what was in them. I wanted only to try to forget, to work it through in my own way. The last thing I needed was to be plunged headlong back into the worst of it on a daily basis.

To start with, I admit, it was hard. I saw a doctor once, but only because the investigating judge had ordered it. If it had been up to me, I wouldn't have gone. Next they wanted some hair, in order to analyse the drugs I had been given. They found traces of sleeping pills and other stuff, though barely enough to show up, it seemed, and certainly not enough to turn me doolally, as some people would later claim. The hair analyst was actually called to give evidence to say that I'd been given so little, a cat would barely have keeled over.

When the mayor came to see me, I took the opportunity of asking my illustrious visitor if he could get some street lighting installed in the famous road by the stadium where it all began, as hundreds of children use it to go to school. I was gratified to learn that two or three weeks later the lights were up and running. But it makes you think: it took what happened to me to get this done.

During the second round of interviews, I got to meet Michel Dumoulin again, the hero of the hour, according to the press. They were right: it was he who had got the bastard to confess, he who'd put him through the mangle. He had explained certain things to me at the time, things I forgot more or less immediately, perhaps because I had to. But one thing I've never forgotten: that this man really is my saviour. It was only after the trial, when we met up again all those years later, that he told me how he had managed to extract the confession.

The cretin had such a high opinion of himself that he was

finally betrayed by his own vanity. Michel had interrogated him at an auspicious moment, he explained. The nerd, a drug addict, had already shopped him, so the bastard really had nowhere to run. But Michel felt he was holding back on something, something that he might be persuaded to offer up if there was a sweetener. 'You know how things work around here,' he said, flattering the bastard with the idea that he might even be one of them. 'If I had anything to play with, well, I might even be able to pull a few strings.' Because things weren't looking too hot for him, and what with the nerd having shopped him, they could just lock him up and throw away the key.

At that stage he was only being interrogated about Laetitia's disappearance, and there was no escaping that. Since there had been several cast-iron witness reports, he would really have needed to pull a fair-sized rabbit out of the hat. When Michel's offer made him feel once again in control, the demon conjuror came out with his lordly statement.

'What if I gave you two girls?'

Michel told me that he'd been utterly stunned. 'We had only been looking for Laetitia, so why had he said two? I took a moment to get my thoughts together, and in the interrogation room there was a photo of you. So I asked him if it was you that he meant. And he said Yes, that Laetitia wasn't alone and that he'd give us the keys to the house in Marcinelle and show us himself where you were hidden.' I suppose the braggart must have had to explain how we wouldn't move a muscle or let out a peep, being far too afraid unless the master himself was there; we would respond to his voice, and his alone.

I had waited many years to talk to Michel. I had kept myself well away from the whole gruesome business, its tentacles seemingly reaching into every part of Belgian life. He had been pulled off the case midstream, a fact I still find very distressing. I admire this man, his work, his impartiality and his rigour. He was one of those who saw through that manipulating, puffed-up psychopath from the start. He refused to play the bastard's game. The bastard was not, as he liked to make out, an insignificant cog in an all-powerful network whose names included the highest in the land. This small-time Macchiavelli lies as easily as he breathes. He puts forward plots and theories as Byzantine as they are pathetic, and my only wish is for them to choke him to death. When I think that he has children, that his wife was complicit, that she waited years before confessing her own role, while little girls died in misery and loneliness, that bodies were even buried in her garden! These people are not people. There is no word blunt enough for them. His name is Marc Dutroux, hers is Michèle Martin – but for me they will always remain nameless.

Why Madame Martin rather than Madame Dutroux? Perhaps it didn't appeal, having to share the name of a man whose criminal record was as horrendous as it's possible to imagine; to share the name of a sexual pervert who had been pursuing his despicable career since the eighties. He had been sentenced to thirteen years for rape and other sexual offences, but freed on 8 April 1992 for 'good conduct', even though both the psychologist and the public prosecutor had been against it. So he'd sworn that next time around, he wouldn't get caught. And for four years – with the connivance of his wife and a spaced-out drug addict – he had succeeded. The official label is 'psychopath'.

At the age of twelve, the word meant nothing to me, and even now, at twenty, I still don't really understand what goes on in a mind like that. All I know is that I wanted to see this 'psychopath' face to face, eyeball to eyeball. When I was twelve, they stopped me, no doubt for my own protection. I had to wait a full eight years to finally have the chance.

And this time it was he who was forced to lower his eyes.

CHAPTER 8

A little personal therapy

The investigating judge wanted me to see a psychiatrist, so I went. I have a vague memory of having to look at some stupid drawings I was supposed to react to. The whole thing was ridiculous and I couldn't think of anything to say. Whenever the subject of psychiatrists came up again, I said no. I didn't want to talk about it. Yes, it had happened, but I wanted it out of my daily life. It was all still there somewhere at the back of my head – nothing could change that – but if I let anyone poke around in there, the inevitable questioning would only stir things up again.

The general view was that I was ill. I was probably in shock, but I wasn't ill. When talking about me, people would say, 'She's got her feet on the ground,' and that's probably true. You can't rewrite history, and I know I can never wipe out what happened, but the best medicine is just to get on with your life and sort it out yourself. At the time, no one understood that.

I knew I needed to put up the shutters. My lawyer, Maître Rivière, was the one person who saw the wisdom in this. I never actually talked to him face to face as, in legal terms, I was a minor, so all communication relating to the case was conducted through my parents. (In Belgian law, victims are as much a part of a trial as the accused and are represented in court by counsel.) In fact, my parents and my sisters were the ones who needed a psychiatrist, not me: all of them ended up having years of therapy, so they were the last people I could confide in. Nor could I talk to friends my own age, who simply wouldn't have understood what I was talking about. They were still very much twelve-year-old girls. I too was a twelve-year-old girl, but with a take on the world of someone much, much older. In my head I was already about eighteen. So my only option was to look after myself, and take out a subscription to my own personal therapy.

It's how I cope with things to this day. Each time I have a flashback, I'll zap it by thinking of something else. Then there's my mirror therapy. As I'm brushing my hair, or putting on my make-up, I'll talk things through with the person looking back at me. Sometimes I'll voice these thoughts out loud, other times – if there are other people around – to myself. And as soon as I get the feeling that I'm sinking into depression, I just knock it on the head. With the hindsight of the last eight years, I know that being depressed does me no good at all. 'Get a grip, girl,' the mirror person will say. 'You held your nerve back then, so bloody well don't flunk it now.' I know I just have to pull back, and cling to the belief that what happened before will not happen again.

Gradually, I began to construct a protective suit of armour. The best way to stop people interrogating me on what I thought about a TV documentary, say, was to make out I had absolutely no interest in it. If, in reality, I did want to see it, then I could always tape it and watch it later without anyone else knowing. I was lucky in that means were found within the family to give me a level of independence, which in practical terms meant a room of my own, up in the attic, with my own television. I could shut myself away, talk to the person in the mirror, think what I wanted, laugh or cry if I wanted, or say and do nothing if I wanted. I had peace and quiet. And if anyone said, 'Did you see that article in the newspaper?' I would say, 'No, I was watching a film on TV.' Sometimes it was even true.

But it took time to learn how to protect myself and, in the early days in particular, it was very hard. When they found the bodies of Julie and Melissa between 15 and 17 August, I hadn't yet taught myself how to turn it all off. The two little girls had died when the bastard was on remand for some petty crime. While he was inside, he'd got his wife to bring them food and water. Or that was the idea. In fact she hadn't, claiming she'd been too frightened to open the massive concrete door. So by the time the monster had returned, Julie and Melissa were dead and 'all he could do' was bury them in his garden.

Then on 3 September two more bodies were found. An and Eefje were dug up from near the chalet belonging to his wheeler-dealer accomplice. Both the girls had been 'asleep' when they'd been buried, but actually still alive, just like the accomplice himself, who was found buried next to Julie and Melissa.

Each time, I found myself asking: *What if it had been me? Where would they have found my body? Which garden would mine have been in?* Later, during the trial, when the abduction and murder of the other girls was being dealt with, I stayed away. I didn't want to make it worse for their parents by showing up, still very much alive. To be the survivor of a massacre isn't easy, either.

Meanwhile, back at home, I was at risk of being suffocated by my mother's concern: 'You can't go out without your sister. You can't go to the shops on your own. You can't cycle to school – at least not yet.' *Why can't they just leave me alone!* a voice screamed inside. *Stop doing my head in about what's been on TV, stop comparing the size of headlines in the newspapers. Let me go to school. Let me live my life. As for the monster and the investigation, let the grown-ups sort it out!* Unfortunately for me, there was little else to read or watch: the Monster of Belgium was wall-to-wall.

School was my saving grace. The headmaster came to see me just before the end of the holidays to ask when I wanted to go back. 'At the beginning of term,' I said, though it seemed an odd sort of question.

'Are you sure?' he said. 'Wouldn't you rather have a day or two more at home, as you missed out on the school holidays?'

So I explained that if I came back later than the others, I'd be like a new girl who didn't know what was what, and it would give people more of an excuse to stare at me. Given my hopeless maths grades, I'd been worried I might be kept down a year. But he quickly put my mind at rest: I'd be going straight up with the rest of my class, he told me. And that perked me up no end.

The outcome of the headmaster's visit was a pep talk that he gave to the whole school. It must have worked, because no one – neither pupils nor teachers – ever asked me a single question. Children are naturally sensitive about not prying into each other's lives. In their world, everything is much more straightforward and if something upsets someone, then you don't talk about it. It's as simple as that. As for finding out what had happened to me, they'd already had their fill from newspapers and TV, not to mention their parents. They could see perfectly well that all I wanted was to carry on as usual and to put the other thing completely behind me. They knew because I had told them, if not in so many words. My class had wanted to give a party a couple of weeks after I got back. I understood why – after all, they'd joined in the search for me like everyone else and they were pleased to see me back. But I said No. I didn't feel like celebrating. Instead, they gave me one of the Missing posters, which they all signed. And at least they could see I wasn't a mass of scabs and scars.

'Weird, that,' I remember one of them saying. 'All that time looking for you and in the end, you weren't that far away!'

'Yeah, weird – but there you go!' I wasn't in the business of handing out details. Anything they knew they'd got from the press.

During the first few days, when reporters and camera crews had come to the house, my father had dealt with them all while I kept my head down. They seemed to get the message, Maître Rivière having made it clear that I was not to be harassed. My father gave one interview to the local paper but, apart from a few pictures the day I returned, of the 'little Sabine returns to the bosom of her family' variety, that was about it. Gradually, silence began to settle around me like a thick fog. No journalists, no statements, no interviews.

Then one day, a few months later, I was outside the house with my dog Sam, busy clearing snow from the front path when I spotted this man wielding a camera over the rose bushes. I told him quite calmly that watching a girl brushing snow from a doorstep would be nearly as interesting to viewers as watching paint dry. That evening, the footage he'd taken was shown on the local news, and I was in fits. The star was Sam, who kept darting in and out of the door. It had been quite windy that day and, as he's part cocker-spaniel, his little ears were flapping up and down as if he was about to take off!

I taped the programme just to have a record of Sam looking so unbelievably cute.

Much later, in 1998, one of my teachers – or it might even have been a pupil – stopped me in the corridor and asked if I'd heard the news.

'Aren't you frightened?'

What news? Frightened?

'He's escaped.'

At first I thought it must be a joke, but then I went outside and seeing the helicopters circling above my head realised it could just be true. If I was frightened, it was only for a split second – I knew he'd have to be exceptionally stupid to come within a million miles of me. Nevertheless, the police had uniformed officers patrolling the school, and they even installed a bodyguard at our house. But by the time I got back from school, he'd gone. The Great Escape was already over.

I read the details in the newspaper like everyone else. He had apparently been at the court in Neufchateau, to consult his file. He'd managed to knock out one policeman, punch another to the ground and somehow grab a gun which, as it turned out, wasn't even loaded. Then he'd stolen a car and screeched off followed by half the local police force, finally holing up in some wood before being ignominiously recaptured by a forest warden! I saw him on the news that night, looking the complete plonker, with his head poking out from the undergrowth and his hands up. But however laughable it may have been, I remember thinking: *If the police don't get*

their act together better than this, it'll be years before the investiga-
tion actually gets to court.

Suddenly it was open season on Sabine Dardenne. As the
media pack drew closer, I dug myself in, deeper and deeper.
My lawyer sent out the message again: No press. Leave her
alone. Luckily I was still a minor: at least on this level I had
some protection, and Maître Rivière confirmed that there was
no reason whatever to get involved with any of the preliminary investigation procedures.

But to return to October 1996. I had only been back at
school for a few weeks when it was announced that a national
demonstration was going to be held on 20 October. It became
known as the White March – 'white' being the symbol of purity
and innocence – a protest march for Belgium's missing or murdered children. The prime mover was the mother of Elisabeth
Brichet, together with the parents of Julie and Melissa. An and
Eefje's parents stayed out of the limelight – in fact, I don't
know if they were even there. Elisabeth Brichet had been
twelve when she went missing on 20 December 1989. At the
time of the White March no one knew what had happened to
her. Her body was only found in 2004, fifteen years after her
disappearance, and not long afterwards Fourniret was arrested.
A French monster this time, who had crossed the border into
Belgium in search of his prey: Elisabeth was found buried in a
chateau in northern France.

The slogan of the White March was: 'Never again'. The

demonstrators also used the occasion to protest against the dismissal of the investigating magistrate, Judge Connerotte, the man in the Hawaiian shirt whom everyone considered had been doing a good job. This 'disciplinary measure', known by everyone as Spaghetti-gate, was the result of the judge having had supper with the families of the victims. By chance I'd happened to turn up, having spent the afternoon with Laetitia, and the judge and I didn't exchange a single word. But the damage was done. He was accused of partiality for having shared a bowl of spaghetti with the people who were parties to the case (victim-plaintiffs) who would be suing the bastard for compensation once he'd been found guilty, which is standard procedure under Belgian law. I should point out that Judge Connerotte's replacement, Judge Langlois, had nothing to do with the decision to sack him. But at the time all this happened, I was far too young to understand the machinations of the Belgian judicial system.

As for the march, I had been determined to go along. 'It was you who wanted to go,' Maître Rivière recently reminded me. 'Your parents thought that the crowds, the television and press from all over the world, would all be too much for you.'

As it turned out, they were right. But at the time, their attitude made me see red, and I'd yelled, 'If you really want to stop me, you can always lock me in the cellar!' It was only two months since I'd emerged from that other cellar but, as all my class were going on the march, my parents had to accept the inevitable, and in the end the whole family went, together with my friends from the estate, neighbours, and the rest of them. It has been estimated that three hundred thousand people converged on Brussels that day. I thought it would be a kind of vigil, where I could join with others in mourning the girls who had died, but it wasn't.

There were so many people, I could hardly breathe. A paramedic nurse walked beside me all the way, and she kept asking me whether I wanted a puffer or a pill. I didn't want anything other than to stay on my feet, I told her. If I was short of breath, it was because of the crowd, and people staring at me as if I was some weird circus animal. In fact, the whole thing felt strange. The march was held to honour the missing children, but also to celebrate Laetitia's and my survival. So our position with regard to the other families was – to put it mildly – tense. Yes, I was alive, but that didn't mean I wasn't affected by the death of the other girls.

The noise of the crowd, and people coming up and kissing me for no reason, staring at me as if they'd seen a ghost, were horrible. I wasn't the heroine of this macabre story, and neither was Laetitia. We were hemmed in so completely that we couldn't make our way through the jostling crowd with their placards and their white balloons, and little white cardboard hats printed with the names of Belgium's abducted children: Julie and Melissa, An and Eefje – found buried. Elisabeth and little Loubna – still missing. Sabine and Laetitia, alive and kicking. I felt very uncomfortable.

All the families were supposed to meet up on the podium,

but we nearly didn't make it and had to be strong-armed through by the police. And there, up on that stage in front of the mass of people, I lost it. I managed to get three words into the microphone, and then my voice cracked. The next day, my photo was in a magazine in the form of a giant poster. In tears.

I hadn't wanted that. I had gone on the march to demonstrate my support, not to demonstrate my grief, and certainly not to be photographed crying in public. For me, crying has always been a very private thing. And I think my hostility towards the press stems from that day. To see myself in close-up, against a backdrop of that huge crowd, knowing that I was now a target for the world's paparazzi, was unbearable. So I did the only thing I could. I disappeared from public gaze.

If I was to keep sane, I decided, I had no real alternative. But it gave rise to the ridiculous idea that I had become a recluse. 'She never leaves the house . . . She's completely beyond reach . . . She has no memory of what happened . . . caused by the high doses of the drugs she was given . . . She was seen at this place: he had handed her over to the network . . .' Luckily, I was totally oblivious to this rubbish.

Shortly after the White March, we were all invited to meet the Prime Minister and take part in a round-table discussion, or so we were told. But there was no round-table discussion. Laetitia and I talked to each other, while the politicians spoke to the parents. It was there that Elisabeth Brichet's mother gave me a photograph of her daughter, telling me how much I resembled her. 'You remind me of her,' she told me. 'She was twelve as well.' I found it incredibly upsetting to be alive, and standing there in front of her. Mrs Brichet had been searching for her daughter since 1989, hoping the various leads would bring some kind of resolution, but without any definite news, she could not even mourn, being pulled this way and that by hope and despair. Perhaps she thought that 'our' monster might have been equally guilty of her daughter's abduction and would one day admit it. But as it turned out it wasn't him; it was the French monster, Fourniret. Obviously there is no scale of monstrousness among psychopaths, but at least Elisabeth died quickly. Not tortured, month after month, slowly sealing her own fate.

As for 'our' monster, he refused to come clean. Julie and Melissa? 'That wasn't me, it was Lelièvre.' (The nerd who was his accomplice when I was kidnapped.) 'It was my wife who let them starve.'

An and Eefje? 'I didn't kill them, that was Weinstein! I only gave them something to sleep.'

Weinstein? 'I didn't kill him.' Weinstein (whom I had never come across) had been found buried beside Julie and Melissa. An and Eefje had been found at Jumet in the garden of a house belonging to this very same Weinstein.

These are only some of the numerous yarns the bastard spun during the long years of the preliminary investigation. But his wife, after years of complicity in his dread deeds, accused him unequivocally. He returned the compliment by begging her to tell the truth! He had only been protecting her from the evil machinations of the imaginary criminal network, he explained, for the sake of the family. This woman was his accomplice. She didn't blink an eye or shed a tear before they picked her up. Yet she knew everything. That she was a mother herself defies belief. Another monster, this time in skirts.

However, on 20 October 1996, the day of the White March, I knew none of this. All I wanted was to lend my support to the parents who had lost a child, the parents who had just buried a child, the parents who were still searching. Yet how could I make things easier for them? I was living evidence of their distress. It was unbearable.

However, I had no room for any more guilt. My childhood had already been destroyed. I was no longer like other innocent girls my age, and yet I craved the anonymity that being among them gave me.

The years between fifteen and nineteen were the most difficult of my life. It's not an easy time for anyone, and I suspect that even if what happened to me hadn't happened, my adolescence would have been fraught.

In terms of my family, I had always felt myself to be an outsider. I was convinced that my parents had never wanted me, that my birth was an 'accident'. If this was a joke, it was one that backfired, because I took it literally, communication never having been a strong point in our family.

162

Apart from being an 'accident', all I knew was that I'd been born between three and four in the morning. My mother couldn't tell me the exact time as she was under anaesthetic, and they hadn't allowed my father to be there for the Caesarean. I found her vagueness far from satisfactory. I've always been obsessive about detail. In the rat-hole I would go mad watching the clock: hours, minutes, seconds. My mother also told me that I was put in an incubator as soon as I was born because I was premature. And that I had a full head of hair. That was it: the sum total of all I knew relating to my beginning. As for the expression on her face, it was like: So what more do you want me to tell you?

That she loved me, perhaps? Or what about how old I was when I took my first step? Or started talking? The kind of things that confirm a child in his or her existence. Instead, I had a residual memory that I hadn't been alone in there. That there'd been another pocket where another baby should have been, but that it had been empty. I never asked my mother about this, because asking her a question was like throwing a coin down a well. You never even heard the splash.

This is only one illustration of the chasm that lies between us, a chasm that has existed ever since I can remember. Perhaps that's why I've always had so many friends outside the family – and why I'm such a chatterbox. Nobody could accuse me of non-communication! If I have children myself, then I'm determined not to make the same mistake. I wouldn't want to muscle in where I wasn't wanted, but I'd always make sure I was there for them when they needed me.

In short, what I wanted from my mother was to be loved for who I was. Perhaps not as she loved her favourite – I couldn't have stood that kind of suffocation in any case – but in the sense, perhaps, of acknowledging my existence. Did it take my disappearance to make her notice me? I still wasn't the favourite, of course, the one whose hair she'd stroke while watching television, the one who looked just like her, and who was such a star at school. I was still rubbish at maths. My bizarre talent for remembering telephone numbers and car registration plates had failed to rub off on anything else (as I was always being reminded). Whereas my sisters had both been straight A students from the year dot. For a brief while, I became the focus of my mother's attention, but it was over before it began. In the short term I was overprotected, but things soon returned to how they'd always been. Maternal tenderness was not something I was about to experience.

'Failed again, I see . . . Didn't I tell you to give the floor a sweep? . . . That bloody dog does nothing but shed hairs . . .' Sometimes I saw myself again in the rat-hole, thinking about my hopeless maths grades, itemising the rest of my faults and painstakingly writing 'I promise to be nicer and to do what I'm told'. It only needed my mother to tell me to get a move on with the sweeping (and this was an order, to be done at the double) and I was back there again, in that hovel where the evil bastard had got me to wash his filthy floor on all-fours, armed only with a disgusting old rag and washing-up liquid. A post-modern Cinderella, in circumstances that no non-pervert could believe possible. Is it any wonder that I took exception to any form of coercion or restraint? Authority and I were not on speaking terms.

Before I was kidnapped, household tasks had never been that big a deal; I suspect I'd been too young to realise what my older sisters must have been doing. I would play with toy cars, go roller-blading, skate-boarding, I kicked a football around and went camping in proper tents, with my friends. I would hang around with my father. I had my little patch of garden – I adore radishes – and when I wanted to duck out completely, then there was always my shed. The fact that my mother didn't communicate with me was neither here nor there. Consciously at least, I wasn't bothered. I'd go out, enjoy myself and when I got back, I'd sulk a bit, and then carry on as usual. But when I'd found myself imprisoned by that psychopath, I'd had the time to mull things over in a way I'd never done before. And going through my school report, counting the days off my calendar, I'd heard my mother's accusatory voice:

'What's this, Sabine? Failed again, I see.' She was always getting at me. And yet she was the one I was writing to. The one person in all the world I wanted to see again. If the bastard had said I could choose just one person out of my family, it would have been her, or my grandmother.

As far as my adolescence was concerned, I began to realise that things had been better when she hadn't bothered with me. Lack of communication in our family had created a fault

line and, when the earthquake arrived, the family just collapsed in on itself.

For the two years that followed my release, I managed to
hold out against the incursions of my family. But things came
to a head when I refused (again) to see a psychiatrist, while
they seemingly spent their entire time in this or that consulting room. Every single discussion on every single subject
ended with the same sentence: 'Sabine, you've got to see a
psychiatrist.'

And I asked myself how it was possible that nobody in the
family had taken a blind bit of notice of me until I'd come
within a whisker of death. That August evening when I was
lifted over the roses into the safety of my own home, if I'd
thought for one moment that I could have been comforted by
my mother, then of course I would have confided in her. But
it wasn't going to happen. Perhaps unconsciously, my silence
became a kind of revenge, as I sometimes made all too clear:
'You've never wanted to tell me anything, so now you know
what it's like.'

The decision not to let my mother read the letters, however, was more considered. She had been very ill with cancer
and had only recently come through a heavy course of
chemotherapy. To pile my own unhappiness on top of her
own misery seemed wrong. Those letters had been written in
desperation and loneliness. And although they had been
addressed to her, I really didn't think I'd ever see her again. I
believed honestly – and still do – that they would be too

painful for her to read. Too painful for me, too. I didn't want to see the look on her face that I would recognise as shame.

It was, perhaps, an exercise in damage limitation. But she should have understood that I was protecting her, if protecting myself at the same time. In place of that, it seemed to me that she was seeking to appropriate my pain, though not in order to ease the weight of it. It was as if she wanted to have the whole experience photocopied onto her. I didn't get it: my suffering was my suffering and nobody else's.

Of course anyone can try to empathise with another person's pain. But no amount of compassion can equate with living it in the flesh. And suffering something from the outside, as my family obviously did, is entirely different. The difference between the sea and the shore.

I experienced the difference myself during the trial. There were people in the court, and there were people in the public gallery. But the people in the gallery were not going through what the people in court were going through. I was in the gallery.

I've met women all too ready to say they know what it must have been like for me. But you can't know what you've never experienced. Ask the same question of any woman who's been raped, and she'll say the same thing.

I don't underestimate what my mother went through. Night after night with no sleeping, just waiting and waiting. And I know too that her health was not good. But she wasn't there in that dark hole, or in the Calvary room, and she wasn't twelve years old. The chasm between her and me was already so wide that, when the earthquake came, it could only get wider.

It was the same when my parents finally separated. Their marriage had been over a long time before lawyers were involved. And it didn't happen – as has been suggested by psychiatrists – as a result of my abduction. My parents can't hide behind me to justify their divorce, any more than experts can hide behind their theories to justify my behaviour.

Everyone was on at me to sort my head out. But I said no. Over and over again. Seeing a psychiatrist would do me no good at all. No one could remove what was in my head. Trying to off-load it onto someone else would be pointless.

In a small country like Belgium, it's impossible to remain anonymous. No matter where I went, everyone knew exactly who I was. The need to protect myself from the looks I got given was another reason for wanting to opt out of the whole hideous business.

There were two major varieties of look. First, there was the pitying kind: 'Oh you poor little thing, I know how you must feel. Here, give me a hug.' Pity I emphatically did not need. Then there was the 'imagining' kind. And those I could not take at all. It would have been bad enough for a grown-up woman, but for a child (which is what I was) – a mere pawn in this sick game of chess that had taken over national life – well, it made me feel like a pariah. I couldn't escape these looks even in my own home. So I just cut myself off, a hard thing to do when you're all cooped up under the same roof.

The only person I felt comfortable with was my grandmother, the one fixed star on my horizon. I didn't deserve her. I hadn't shown her enough affection when I'd had the chance, but I didn't know how to until it was all too late. My mother, being a nurse, never had a 9–5 job, so my grandma had been much more hands-on than she would otherwise have been. If my mother was on an early shift, for example, she'd drop me off at Grandma's on her way in to work. It would then be Grandma who'd give me breakfast and drive me to school, picking me up at midday again to take me back to her house for lunch. My mother would collect me from there at 4.00. If she was on a 'late', it would work the other way around; I'd be dropped off at Grandma's at 4.00 for supper and homework. Sometimes she would even put me to bed, and my mother would have to wake me up to go home.

When it came to homework, my grandmother's attitude was the polar opposite to my parents'. She would always try to help, though obviously that got more difficult as I got older. But even so, whatever the subject, she would sit down beside me and just watch as I worked, genuinely interested in whatever it was I was doing. There was no 'Do this . . . Now that . . . No, no, not like that.' She would just say, 'Now you just make a start, and if you need any help, we'll see what your old grandma can do.'

I would eat my bread and jam, unpack my satchel and

happily set to work. And if I didn't understand something, I'd only have to look up and Grandma would be there, no matter how long I took. Whereas at home it was: 'So, were you planning to finish your homework this year or next?'

My grandmother died when she was eighty-six and I was fifteen, and it filled me with anger, pain and regret. Why hadn't I gone to live with her? Why hadn't I gone to see her more often instead of hanging around with my friends? The rest of the family were particularly conscientious in their visits, and I couldn't bear it when they'd get back and tell me how they'd been talking about me. I don't even make up for it now by visiting her grave on All Saints' Day, but then you don't have to be doubled up beside a tombstone in order to grieve.

That dear kind old lady who loved me and didn't expect anything from me . . . if only she could have waited a little bit longer, then I would have talked to her. She knew how to listen, and she would have calmed and soothed me and made me feel whole. I will thank her, one day. But I was only fifteen, and I fucked up.

I yearned to be with people my own age. I wanted people to laugh with, dance with, chatter with till all hours of the morning. I wanted to live.

When I was about sixteen I met a boy. He was a bit older than me, just one of the gang I used to hang around with. I never talked about what had happened to anyone. For nearly four years, I'd cut myself off from it all, and managed to live a life much like anybody else. Naturally I rebelled against my parents, who still tried to stop me going out late. But on the whole I led what might be thought of as the normal life of a normal adolescent. There was no more talk of the case on television, I had even given up my own personal therapy – it had done its job. I was just a teenager, although I felt older than my contemporaries, and above all different. Most importantly I never thought about 'him', and if I came across something in the press, I didn't even bother to read it.

But when I started going around with this boy, the relationship with my parents went from bad to worse. Although he was genuinely nice – and at that stage no more than a friend – they saw things differently: one good-for-nothing (my school reports were still making my mother wince) consorting with another good-for-nothing.

It was always going to happen. Like any other girl, sooner or later I would fall in love and it was something I both feared and needed. What I didn't need was to have to do battle with my family at the same time. Falling in love is a serious business, especially when you're sixteen. And that's how old I was when it happened. We'd skirted around the subject, squabbling like children, because when it came to being stubborn, I had finally found my match, and usually it was me who gave in. I still hadn't told him that I loved him even if it was as obvious as the nose on my face.

Like everyone else in Belgium, he knew what had happened to me, but we had never talked about it. And now here we were . . .

Somehow I managed to raise the subject. I knew I had to. 'You probably realise,' I began, 'that this could be difficult for me.' Then – more nervous than I'd ever seen him before – he admitted that he didn't exactly know what to do either. And that was the best thing that could possibly have happened.

'Perfect,' I said. 'We'll just have to muddle through together!'

And so we did. Without a backward glance I had leaped the bonfire that had threatened to turn my future to ashes. Only love could have achieved this magical deliverance.

It was never going to be a happy-ever-after relationship as far as he was concerned – although I have to admit I thought it would be. And so another river was crossed: my first broken heart. I was devastated, which was probably inevitable.

But at least, from beginning to end, it was love. And I threw myself into it as willingly as I have ever thrown myself into anything. As for the psychopath, he has never loved. He doesn't know the meaning of it, or even that it exists.

I may not have been the best pupil the school ever turned out, but I passed the final exams without a problem. College or university wasn't really an option – my mother's financial situation put paid to that. So, like dozens of school leavers before me, I set out down a trail of badly paid, nothing jobs going nowhere, until finally I found something that wasn't that great, but at least was steady. When things at home reached rock bottom, I was able to move out and get my own place.

It did me a lot of good, slamming my parents' front door for the last time. From my teddies to my illusions, I left everything behind. Only the stroppy little madam came with me. She'd served me well and I knew I'd be needing her to build my new life.

And whenever things get me down – and they do – I know that nothing can ever be as bad as then. The one positive thing that emerged from the rat-hole was self-esteem: little by little, I came to recognise what I had achieved. *You never gave in, and you stayed alive.* That I am harder as a result is undoubtedly true. Many people see that as something negative, but I prefer to see it as something positive, a protective shell, something that has enabled me to meet life head on. While many people find my black humour shocking, it allows me to laugh at anything, particularly 'Belgium's premier psychopath': poor little Marc-y.

When I emerged from the hole I told myself I was not going to break down, and for eight long years I succeeded. There's only one way to get over something like this and that's to keep your nerve when you're up against it. I didn't crack up when I was freed from the monster's grip at the age of twelve.

But when I turned twenty, another severe test of nerve awaited me. This time I was really going to be up against it: face to face with the man they'd refused to let me see when I was twelve.

CHAPTER 9

'D the Damned'

Maître Rivière says that he met me twice when I was twelve, but I have no memory of it at all. Nor did I know that, even before he'd been officially appointed to act for me, he'd been helping the investigation on a voluntary basis. He had suggested to the police that he patrol the roads around the motorway interchange near our house on his motorbike, checking out the warren of lay-bys and underpasses where junkies and the homeless tended to hang out.

Shortly after my eighteenth birthday, he suggested we meet up to discuss whether I wanted to continue the line that had been agreed with my parents: no press and a total embargo on any incursions into my private life. From now on all such decisions would be up to me. He would also keep me up to date on new developments – which had not been the case before, when my parents would come back from meetings with him and refuse to tell me what had been discussed. I took strong exception to this. After all, it was my life they were talking about. As a result, I had no clear idea as to how the case itself was evolving, particularly in relation to the theory that had gained considerable popular currency, namely that Dutroux – 'the Damned' – was a mere middleman in a vast network of child-prostitute procurement. The legal teams, like the country at large, were now split into two very different camps, one of which believed that the investigation had been hindered, if not directly sabotaged, by highly placed individuals who, in effect, had been protecting 'their man'.

Two further names had now been added to the list of accused: along with Lelièvre (the nerd in the hat) and Michèle Martin (wife), we now had Weinstein and Nihoul. Weinstein, a former armed robber, had returned to Belgium in 1992 following his release from a French prison. He lived in the chalet in Jumet where the bodies of An and Eefje – who'd been drugged and buried alive – were recovered from the garden.

Basically this Weinstein and 'd the d' had been running a stolen-car operation. Now his former partner was accusing him of a great deal more. It was Weinstein who had decided to get rid of the girls, 'd the d' swore; his own role was merely to 'put them to sleep' before Weinstein buried them alive. Weinstein was unable to confirm or deny this allegation as, by now, he too was dead, his body having been found in the garden of another of Dutroux's houses in Sars-la-Buissière, beside those of the two little eight-year-olds, Julie and Melissa.

So who had killed Weinstein, then?

Dutroux swore that he had absolutely no idea . . .

The other new member of the cast was Nihoul. He, at least, was still alive. He had also been involved in the car-stealing racket. It was to Nihoul, Dutroux swore, that he was supposed to deliver the girls – once he had done with them himself. As for the 'secret place' at the Marcinelle house, that was just a staging post, a holding pen where child prostitutes destined for the paedophile ring would be kept before transferring them to Nihoul. It turned out that Nihoul had indeed been trafficking in prostitutes, though the court accepted that he'd never put so much as a toe into the murky waters of paedophilia. According to the original investigation team, which is to say Michel Dumoulin and his colleagues – my true saviours – this version of events just didn't stand up.

As for me, the surviving witness, I could only talk about my eighty days and nights. Dutroux was the only person I had ever seen, apart from the nerd Lelièvre, who had certainly participated in my abduction and also muttered unconvincing confirmation of the pervert's underworld-gang scenario: how my father had done the dirty on the big boss and then refused to pay the ransom. But that was all. Nihoul – neither the man nor the name meant anything to me.

The story of the big bad boss was designed simply to keep me in a state of terror, with the added advantage of casting my persecutor into the role of 'saviour', the mirror opposite of the truth. I would die if I refused to be raped. I would die if I made any noise. In fact I lived under permanent sentence of death. No one had paid any ransom because no ransom had been demanded. Exactly the same story had been trotted out for Laetitia. And I have no doubt that it was a well-worn tale, at least for Julie and Melissa. It's unlikely he used it for An and Eefje, however. For a start, they were a good deal older and therefore unlikely to have swallowed it. But also, he didn't speak Dutch, which was their language. It seems that Eefje made two attempts to escape – sadly without success. (She tried to get out through the corrugated plastic roof light, the one the bastard made me 'sunbathe' under.) So that poor girl clearly hadn't bought the gangland-HQ-surrounded-by-gun-toting-heavies story. Dutroux himself admitted that, at the time, there had been four of them in the house at Marcinelle: 'the two little ones in the hiding place and the other two upstairs', and that it was really quite difficult to manage them all.

So the bastard was now playing the concerned parent?

As for his wife – the most appalling of his accomplices, in my view, and arrested at the same time as 'd the d' – the team of investigators was in no doubt. She admitted that she was fully aware of the abductions, the rapes and the rest of it. The reason she failed to denounce him to the police, she claimed, was fear. She went on to accuse 'the love of her life' of everything he himself continued to deny. The kidnappings, she said, were his idea, not Lelièvre's; it was he who had got rid of Weinstein as well as the two older girls. As for the little ones who had been left in her care while Dutroux was in prison, she'd been too afraid to go down to the cellar, though naturally, she had no idea why, when or how they had died.

I took on board the various details bit by bit, but an already complex picture was complicated even further every time Dutroux gave a new twist to his original lies. Yet what became obvious to me was that the paedophile-network story was nothing but a labyrinthine smoke-screen thrown up simply to obscure the bastard's guilt. He had played a similar game in the eighties, when he was found guilty of raping two underage girls. He was, he claimed, 'a wronged man, victim of a miscarriage of justice perpetrated by powerful figures in an attempt to stop the true culprits being identified'. For the rape and sexual abuse of these girls, he had been sentenced in 1989 to thirteen years' imprisonment, but was released on parole just three years later for 'good conduct'. The parole terms included being seen by a psychiatrist along with his wife, who had been found guilty of aiding and abetting the rapes. These sessions with the psychiatrist were both quick and useful. Instead of swallowing the Rohypnol he was given – tranquillisers – he secreted them in his cheeks, thus saving them for future nefarious use. Another interesting detail that emerged from this period of detention was that a fellow inmate had taught him how to build a bolt-hole in a cellar, one that would escape the notice of the most thorough of police searches. This man – a burglar – had testified under oath.

But for many others, the story of the high-level paedophile ring, in which he was but an insignificant link in the chain, was the one they chose to believe.

In 2003, the Dutroux case was finally coming up for trial, the date set for 1 March. All I wanted was to keep well clear of anything that didn't directly concern me: the other strands of the investigation, as they were called. But I would give evidence relating to everything I had lived through, everything I had been forced to endure, and he wouldn't wriggle out of that so easily.

The fact that I was going to be called as a witness at all didn't go down well among the supporters of the paedophile-ring theory. (Under Belgian law, witnesses are selected by the investigating judge rather than by prosecution or defence counsel.) Their contention was that I had been so drugged up that I probably wouldn't remember a thing and that, indeed, the experience had turned me into some kind of gibbering vegetable. 'Are you sure you saw only him?' would be translated as 'This absurd idea of a lone pervert isn't going to get you anywhere, you know.'

Maître Rivière had succeeded in removing from the record a statement that 'even if her memory appeared to be intact, her evidence would be rendered inadmissible as she was permanently under the influence of Rohypnol'.

Maître Rivière worked tirelessly to convince the press

that I had only been drugged for the first few days. I was still keeping clear of the media pack – the only people I talked to were members of the investigative team. My only other contribution to the investigation was a re-enactment of the kidnapping itself, in the company of my own superhero, Michel Dumoulin. However painful for me, I knew it had to be done, but at least the accused wasn't brought in to watch, which he could have been.

In fact Michel and I even got to laugh. It was when we passed a not dissimilar van, with 'The King of Chickens' emblazoned on its side – I've got a copy of the photo that appeared in a local paper. The article went on to reveal that the whole exercise had been very relaxed and that I'd proved to be a cyclist of competition standard! How they knew is beyond me, given that no journalist had set eyes on me since I was twelve.

But, as Maître Rivière and I used to say: if you don't know, you invent. Or they did. Some claimed that the reason I was being kept at arm's length from the media was not that my lawyer was adhering to protocol, but that I was in a permanent drug haze. The way that my evidence was subtly undermined long before I even took to the witness stand was very damaging.

'There's nothing else for it,' my lawyer announced to me one day. 'You're going to have to talk to them.' It was the only way, he decided, to prove once and for all that far from spending eighty days half comatose, I'd been fully conscious and my memory was as good as anybody's.

Which is how I came to face my first press conference. It was held at Maître Rivière's chambers, and about twelve print journalists had been invited to attend. I remember being somewhat tense, even though there were no cameras present. But it was the first time in my life I'd had to face the press in person. It was all very low key, and I soon felt completely comfortable. After it was over, sandwiches and drinks appeared, and they even got a taste of my black sense of humour:

'Which sandwiches are mine?' I asked, turning to my lawyer when the plate was brought in. 'You know, the ones with the Rohypnol in them. Don't let anyone else take them. They're all for me!'

Anyway, they got the idea: I was a clear-headed young woman, who answered their questions precisely and with no trace of the loony I'd been made out to be. If there'd been anyone else at all in that hovel, I'd have noticed, just as I noticed everything else.

The investigation team, Michel Dumoulin and his colleagues, men for whom I have enormous respect, both because they literally freed us and because of the work that they had already done, never had a moment's doubt as to the truth of my testimony. They were the ones who had gathered Laetitia and me up in their arms that August afternoon, and they knew exactly what state we were in. Shocked, yes, but clear-headed enough to want to beat the living daylights out of the paedophiliac bastard. Laetitia had been there six days, for three of them heavily drugged – all of which I could confirm, but obviously having spent two and a half months cooped up with the monster I was going to have more to say than her. Yet since the earthquake that had shaken our small country to the core eight years previously, every good citizen of Belgium appeared to have their own idea of the truth. In streets, in cafés, in the train or the underground, the talk was of nothing else. The case hadn't even come to trial, yet already fifteen books had been published. My parents had boxes full of newspapers they'd collected – I'd even helped pile them up myself, without the strength to sort or read them. My own catalogue of events and the flashbacks that continued to take me unawares were enough. I just had to stay centred, to live my life and turn my back on anything that threatened to disturb my equilibrium.

As soon as the date of the trial was announced, I knew that it would only be a matter of days before I'd be plunged back into the stinking mire. In the media, the background and build-up to the trial were re-hashed *ad nauseam*: the original investigation, the maze of trails that led nowhere, lines of investigation discarded, then later revisited. There were over 400,000 pieces of paper from enquiry and witness statements, to Spaghetti-gate and other sackings, including Michel Dumoulin himself, who had first got the monster to talk and was personally responsible for bringing us out alive. From top to bottom, heads had rolled: the judicial system itself had been called into question, ditto the police service. There were question marks everywhere – from the minister of justice who had gone over the heads of the people on the ground in authorising Dutroux's release in 1992, to the violence that broke out during the White March. Enquiry about enquiry. Investigation into investigation. Year after year after year of doubt.

So at last the moment had arrived, and Belgium waited with baited breath for the truth to be unveiled. Which, given that they were dealing with a psychopath, was a bit optimistic. The weight of it all was too much for me – it was like standing at the base of Everest, I felt so tiny and insignificant. I had no idea at this stage what position Laetitia would take. Much of the trial would be concerned with the other girls and their parents, the victims being part of the whole process in Belgian law, so I felt strangely out of kilter with everyone else, purely because I had survived.

The trial took place in a small town called Arlon, simply because of the kind of crime involved. The courtroom itself could hold no more than the key participants: the three judges, the nine jurors (four one side, five the other). To one side, but at the same level and with the window behind him as tradition decreed, was the public prosecutor. Facing the judges and jury were the lawyers, on the window side were the counsel for the victims, on the other side the counsel for the accused. And lastly, the accused themselves: 'd the d', Martin (wife), Lelièvre and Nihoul.

As the minister of justice announced that the budget for

this fandango of a media trial would amount to four and a half million euros (about three million pounds), the little town braced itself to accommodate hundreds of journalists from across the world. More than 1,300 had requested press accreditation, but as there were only sixteen places available in the press gallery, it would turn out to be a bit like musical chairs. Those without a seat could watch in an adjoining room, where the proceedings were relayed non-stop on video screens until their turn in the gallery came round again. Originally scheduled to last two months, the trial ran from 1 March until 22 June, nearly twice as long as planned.

The victims and their families, with the right to be housed at the court's expense, were put up in a former military barracks. Maître Rivière had decided I needed somewhere a little less public, which suited me very well, since the last thing I wanted was to find myself the prey of photographers.

Three hundred police had been drafted in as security, and the way this small town responded to the invasion was certainly impressive. The fact that only a handful of the public would be allowed in open court I personally found very reassuring, although of course the complaints about reduced access were very loud.

Maître Rivière had envisaged my testimony in two parts. Firstly, the reading of my letters by one of the investigators. This was to avoid my having to answer questions about the precise nature of what I had been forced to undergo, all of which I had written about in sufficient detail. Secondly, I would take the witness stand in person in order to go through the kidnapping, and my 'unusual summer holiday' courtesy of 'd the d'. Unlike in England or America, where witnesses are led through their testimony by their counsel and then cross-examined by the other side, witnesses under Belgian law belong to neither side. They give their evidence and then can be questioned on it by any of the lawyers present, the general prosecutor, the victim-plaintiffs' counsel or the defendants' counsel.

The only remaining question was whether to give my evidence *in camera*, or in open court. I would have preferred to do it in private, but Maître Rivière persuaded me otherwise. 'The jury will already have heard what you wrote in your letters, so you won't have to go through that again – it will be all too clear. But if you do choose to give your evidence in private, people might think you have something to hide.'

And so I did as he advised. I need only be present, he said, at those parts of the trial that directly concerned me. Staying in the same hotel as my lawyers, Maître Jean-Philippe Rivière and Maître Céline Parisse, I would be kept up to speed with what was happening. Once my testimony had been logged by the court, I could then sit with the other victim-plaintiffs and follow the rest of the trial in person. But it would be seven tense weeks before that day arrived. Until then, news would reach me by telephone from different sources, and I would hear things about my torturer that defied belief.

One investigator reported that the monster had

attempted to artificially inseminate his wife. He was desperate to have a daughter, and so he had attempted to put into practice a technique he had read about in some magazine article, which involved putting his sperm into a plastic bag that his wife then had to leave inside her for three or four days. The rationale behind this was that boy spermatozoa died more quickly than girl spermatozoa.

Amongst other scams, less 'scientific' but equally well thought out, he set out to fleece his ancient grandmother of her house and income – this with the help of his wife, whom it turned out he had married in prison.

The rapes at Mons he committed while on compassionate leave. Having obtained early release for 'good conduct', he requested to be registered as an invalid, saying that he had been taken ill while in prison. This made him eligible for invalidity benefit to the tune of 800 euros a month, courtesy of the state.

As I was living on the minimum wage, that made me incredibly angry!

A former inmate of the prison at Mons said – to a journalist, I think – 'He's nothing but a slug.'

A slug, a monster, an ogre, a paedophile, a psychopath. To me he would always be a stinking creep, oily enough to fry chips in. I'd heard that he still stank, yet apparently he'd been complaining about the unhygienic conditions in the cells beneath the courtroom and he would bash his head against the wall as a form of protest. I would have thought that a private cell, with washing and toilet facilities, enough to eat and the possibility of consulting his file, was actually rather more than he deserved. I had something a little less luxurious in mind for him. A hole in the ground, say. A bare six feet in length and under three feet in width, and not high enough to stand up in. Pitch dark, apart from a bright light that you couldn't turn off, with a thin, disintegrating mattress on a cement floor. Mouldy bread, and a chamber pot.

One can but dream . . .

In court he continued to play the superstar, pathetic and ridiculous, without a scrap of humanity or respect for others, without the merest hint of guilt, let alone remorse, offering up disgusting details to the parents of his little victims.

On 15 April, one of the investigators read out to the jury the letters I had written to my family, as well as the one specifically directed to my mother. My two lawyers did not want me to have to go through the sordid details and painful explanations in person, but I was there. Until they were read out, I don't think I fully understood the impact they would have. An unearthly silence filled the court, apart, that is, from the sound of crying. The reality of the Calvary room, the sexual abuse and the suffering it had caused me and which I had innocently described in the letter to my mother when I was twelve years old, were unbearable to listen to. But the jurors had to hear.

After this session, Maître Rivière spoke to the press. 'With the testimony of the living witnesses, the trial has reached its turning point. From here on, there will be no more fobbing off responsibility onto fantasies and ghosts.' As he spoke, I realised that if I had died some time during the previous eight years, it would not have mattered; these letters would have spoken for me.

Fortunately I did make it. A victim, certainly. But a living witness.

CHAPTER 10

Jigsaw

The trial was like a vast, sprawling jigsaw puzzle on a black background. And I was supposed to fit together the pieces – also black – that would represent my eighty days of captivity.

Not everyone was pleased that I had been called to give evidence. I'd heard 'witness' being used as if in quotation marks; 'Mademoiselle Dardenne, or "the witness", as she is called these days'; or 'the case's so-called "living witness"'. While I completely understood the pain suffered by those parents whose children had never come back, the sense of rebuke I felt simply for having survived was harder to accept. Nor could I fathom the affront when my lawyer referred to me as Mademoiselle Dardenne rather than 'little Sabine'.

I was not a dead little girl. I was twenty and I couldn't spend the rest of my life apologising just for being alive. Nor could I remain silent about what had happened. Yet my rejection of the coward's big-wheel network fantasy was treated as a betrayal by the ones who had swallowed it whole. I used to think how much easier it would have been for the parents – and the grotesque quagmire of the trial – had it been legally possible to use a truth serum on this pathological liar. It was not knowing what had happened to their daughters that made it so much more difficult for them to deal with.

Like the other victim-plaintiffs with the right to sue for compensation, my mother and father could have sat in court, but they agreed not to come, both for my sake and for theirs.

I arrived at Arlon the evening before I was due to give evidence. I was a bundle of nerves, and my head was full of questions for my two lawyers. What if the judge asked me something I couldn't remember? Was he an understanding sort of person? And if I had forgotten something, what was to stop me being written off as a loony again?

We were staying in a country house hotel, a little way outside the town in the middle of beautiful parkland. My lawyers had decided that I needed somewhere peaceful away from the media free-for-all. The staff knew who I was, but the journalists were still completely in the dark as to my whereabouts. The hotel was under police guard and everything was very quiet. But just in case I got over-anxious, Maître Parisse had put me in a room just along from hers. It was important, she said, that I get a good night's sleep – 'And for all our sakes, no more questions!' Yet my head was full of them. My lawyers gave me a glass of white wine as a night-cap, bestowing on it medicinal properties. As I never drank anything in the normal course of things, the tension soon melted away.

It felt so strange: although this was the culmination of years of waiting, I felt undaunted. Confronting this monster face to face was what I had always wanted. And lying there, in the moments before I fell asleep, I wondered what I would feel. It wasn't that I thought I might burst into tears or go weak at the knees – I had nothing to fear from him any more. I had seen him on television, in his bullet-proof glass box, in his office-manager suit, his smarmed-down hair, taking down notes like some jobsworth. He was still playing the film star, complaining about conditions in the cells, not letting anyone take 'Monsieur Dutroux's' photograph, whereas he'd had no qualms about snapping chained-up, naked little girls, or filming himself abusing other young girls drugged up to the eyeballs somewhere in Slovakia, or jollifications with his own wife.

Eventually I went to sleep.

The next morning a police driver arrived to take Maître Parisse and me to the court. We had an unmarked car as the press would have recognised Maître Rivière's, and he went on his own. From then on, till the moment I stepped into the witness box, Maître Parisse never left my side, and I can never thank her enough.

The roads leading into the little town were in gridlock, so the driver put a flashing light on top of the roof, and we drove straight down the middle, between the stationary lanes of traffic, the two-tone police horn blaring. It was like being in a film. I chatted away as if this was completely normal, my usual safety valve coming into play.

To get into the building itself, we went in by the back entrance to avoid the eyes of the curious – just like the accused. I'd never been in a court before, and I was like a child again, all eyes, taking everything in, such as the security arch everyone had to walk through, and my bag being searched – no guns or knives, just cigarettes and a lighter.

I caught sight of André Colin, the policeman whom Laetitia had recognised in the cellar the afternoon we got out. That was the last time I had seen him, in fact, and I can remember giving him a huge smile. The sight of a friendly face in this forbidding place felt so reassuring.

'All right?' he whispered.

'So far so good . . . but you'll have to ask me again later!' My jokiness was just a defence mechanism, a way of keeping my true emotions in check; I was determined not to lose my dignity, both for my own sake and other people's.

I was shown to the waiting room reserved for witnesses. As well as me, there were two psychiatrists, a psychoanalyst and an investigative judge from my home town. This was when I had to say goodbye to Maître Parisse, as she wasn't allowed to mix with the other witnesses. So as things began to get under way, I began to chat to the court usher, who told me his name was Jules. He turned out to be a grandfatherly sort of person who was always offering me glasses of water and biscuits. I could see the other witnesses looking at me as if to say, Is it really her? He was so kind that I felt my eyes fill with tears.

It was Jules's job to escort witnesses from the waiting room into the court, and when it was my turn, he directed me to follow him into the corridor. The door into the court was open and, as I caught my first glimpse of the throng of people, I was seized by panic: the press, the parents of the other children, the public gallery, I could see them all. I couldn't go on, but sat down in a chair, feeling a rush of blood to my face. *I'm going to faint*, I thought, *I can't go through with this*.

And then came Jules's firm voice in my ear.

'It's got to be done.'

He took my arm as if I'd been a little old lady, and led me towards the open door. It was as if I was in a trance: my feet moved one after the other, but it wasn't me who was doing it. And then, as I crossed the threshold into the courtroom, suddenly my strength seemed to return, because there, directly in front of me, was the glass box. Face to face: the moment I had been waiting for.

Dutroux, Lelièvre – his henchman, and the other two, whom I'd only seen on television: Michèle Martin and Nihoul. I barely noticed the last one; he looked totally out of place, as if wondering what on earth he was doing there at all. But the other three, I couldn't and wouldn't take my eyes off. Especially him. I hadn't known, even up to the last instant, just how I would feel seeing him again eight years later.

I felt nothing.

He looked older, but just as ugly. He lowered his eyes, but I didn't. I felt like saying, *Look at me, you pathetic piece of shit.* But I was in a court of law, and I was a bit unnerved at the thought of having to speak in front of all these people. If anything, the room was more frightening than he was. I turned my head to nod to Maître Rivière, as if to say: *Don't worry, I won't let you down.*

I was just about to sit down when the principal judge began to speak.

'Sabine Dardenne?'

'Present!' I said, just as if he was taking the register at school. The newspaper reports the next day said that my voice had trembled a bit. But it had nothing to do with fear, even though the whole business – the courtroom itself and the mass of people staring at me – was pretty intimidating. It's to do with the breathing problems I've had ever since I was born, and my voice takes time to get going in the morning.

Maître Rivière had explained how I always had to address everything to the principal judge as it was he who would be asking the questions. If I had a question myself, then I would have to ask through him. This had the added advantage of my not having to look at anyone else. After I'd confirmed my identity, the judge began.

'So you took your bicycle and set off for school. Perhaps you can tell the court what happened next . . .'

I went back through everything again. It was easier than

it might have been, as my letters had already been read out, and when we got to that part the judge asked whether I wanted to go back over it, and I said 'No, not particularly.'

Then Maître Rivière took over. He had three questions that he wanted me to answer in detail for the sake of the jury. He asked me to explain how I'd been forced to clean the house; whether I had watched television with him, and what programmes. I can remember clearly my answer to that one. 'An undecoded satellite porn channel. He said I had to watch it through the fog caused by the lines. I said I didn't see the point, as I'd already experienced it "live".'

I waited for the judge's final question to me, which I knew would come: 'Is there anything else you want to add?' Maître Rivière knew I had a question, a question of my own. A question for the accused. He said I should wait for the judge to say these words. But they didn't come! The judge, it turned out, had simply forgotten. So Maître Rivière said it himself.

I turned to look directly at the accused. I had worked out how to phrase my question via the judge, as I knew I had to. But I never took my eyes off him from the moment I started speaking.

'I would like to ask Marc Dutroux a question, even though I think I can guess his answer. He complained that I behaved like a pig. So why then, didn't he just liquidate me?'

Behind the walls of his see-through prison, I watched as he got up from his chair to answer my question. His head was bowed, he still didn't look at me.

'There was never a question in my mind of liquidating her. That was suggested to her later, after she left the hiding place.'

Framing my words carefully, I replied: 'With this sort of person, that kind of answer is only to be expected.'

I had finished giving evidence. The judge gave me to understand that I was free to go. But as I was about to leave the witness stand, I had the feeling that someone was moving inside the glass box. I'd have put any money on it being the complicit wife and mother. I was right.

'Mademoiselle Dardenne,' she began, 'I would like to apologise.'

My blood froze as I stopped, then turned as if in slow motion. All thoughts of addressing myself to the judge had disappeared.

'You knew where I was, and who I was with, and what I was forced to go through. And to think that you are a mother yourself makes me want to vomit. As for my forgiveness, forget it.'

'I'm sorry now that I didn't go to the police when he snatched Julie and Melissa. I'm not asking you to forgive me, because I know that what happened was unforgivable. And I don't know what you must have gone through because I can't begin to imagine my own children imprisoned like that. But I know I did wrong.'

'Sorry,' I said, not feeling sorry at all. 'I'm just not interested.'

I think that asking us to forgive her – because she went through the same performance with Laetitia a few days later – was an attempt to somehow lessen her own burden of guilt. She'd been involved right from the early eighties. He'd told her everything, and she even allowed this psychopath to father her children. Now that she was separated from him, she would finally realise, I hoped, the enormity of what she had done.

She had let other people's children be raped and starved and now she had the nerve to start talking about her own! Unlike those other parents, she would still get to see her children – her lawyers had won her visiting rights, at least for the littlest ones. And I pity them, shunted round from foster parent to foster parent, living under assumed names, their lives crucified by having such a mother and father. How dare she think that I could ever begin to forgive her!

After I sat down, the public prosecutor summed up.

'Such evidence as we have heard today is an indictment beyond commentary. We can only listen with humility and respect.'

I left the court feeling empty but relieved. It was all over. No more being put in the stocks. And I had won. He hadn't dared look me in the eye. As for what he had said – that weasel would have said anything. I, of all people, never expected him to tell the truth.

The next day – at a session I didn't attend – Dutroux claimed that I was to have been handed over to Nihoul and the 'network'. Later, in my capacity of victim-plaintiff (rather than witness), I asked the judge if the accused could kindly expand on that aspect, as I hadn't quite grasped how it worked.

It seems unlikely that he picked up on the irony in my use of 'kindly'. Behind the glass, he held up his notes – the standard way he avoided eye-to-eye confrontation.

'I should have handed her over to Nihoul's network at the beginning, but I grew fond of her . . .'

The judge cut him short. 'You meant to make good the loss of Julie and Melissa?' Then off he went, an interminable and completely incomprehensible monologue in his usual nasal monotone and the hurt tones of the fall guy who might have raped, but had never killed.

'So am I to thank him,' I asked via the judge, 'for having saved my life?!'

'No. I didn't say that. I know I did wrong.'

But still the question persists. Why didn't he get rid of me? This animal said he had grown fond of me. Could he really think that could win over the jurors? Or me?

Then it was Laetitia's turn. She told the judge that she 'couldn't promise to speak without fear or hate'. And she began to tell her story.

'I was at the local pool, when this van pulls up . . . the guy makes out as if he doesn't understand what I've said, and while that was going on, the other creep pulls me down on the ground and the next moment I'm trussed up like a chicken.'

The judge asked her about the hole.

'How did you manage, with the two of you in there?'

'There was the wall, then Sabine, then me, then the wall.'

'And you were younger and thinner in those days?'

'Are you calling me fat?'

I had to stifle a laugh. This wasn't the worst, though. A juror asked her how come he'd still raped her, if she'd had her period.

I could see that Laetitia was really upset, all alone up there in the witness box. I was tempted to grab the microphone and give this idiot juror a piece of my mind. Didn't they know by now the kind of sexual deviant, the child molester they were dealing with? As if a little detail like that would put the monstrous psychopath off!

I'd seen Laetitia a week after the trial had begun and she hadn't been at all sure that she would be up to giving evidence.

'It's not going to be easy,' I told her. 'But think of it as giving him a punch in the face. You've got to do it.'

So she did. And bravely – she even had a go at him. She wanted to know just how heavily she'd been drugged those first few days. The fact that her memory was so hazy disturbed her as much as anything else did.

'Why did he make me drink the coffee right down to the grounds?' she asked. In other words, had the coffee itself been drugged?

No, he replied. He was in the habit of finishing his coffee

to the last drop. This was perfectly normal, he said. He didn't believe in waste. And for once I don't think he was lying. Because it was perfectly in keeping with what I already knew: he kept the bath water to flush the toilet with, the mouldy bread was never thrown away, he drank the liquid that was in tinned food, did not brush his teeth or waste coffee grounds.

I'll never forget the cruelty of the questions put to Laetitia by his lawyer:

'Did he say to you "the worst I can do to you is force you to make love"?'

'Yes.'

'And he gave you some contraceptive pills?'

'Yes.'

'And you haven't been seen by a psychiatrist?'

'No.'

'So, it would seem then, that you were able to take it in your stride.'

Until that moment I'd had no idea that, like me, Laetitia had decided to pull herself out of the hell on her own. Watching her in the witness box giving her evidence and, even more perhaps, listening to her replies – with the occasional 'I don't know' or 'I can't remember', while trying valiantly to keep herself together in front of this monster – I remembered that moment when I first saw her, chained up to the bunk. And then, down in the hell-hole, I remembered hearing her reply in that woozy voice, when I had wanted to warn her of what might lie in store upstairs in the Calvary room:

'It's already happened.'

She was here because of me. She was having to answer all these cruel bastard questions, to justify what had happened to her, because of me. It was pointless anyone saying that if it hadn't been her, it would have been someone else. I felt sick. I tried to rationalise my way out of my guilt, but I couldn't do it. Even a bare two months after our release, when she and I had met up for the White March, I had tried to exculpate myself.

'Like I told you when you arrived, I'd been locked up with that bastard for seventy-seven days, and hardly a day went by without a visit to the Calvary room, so I was halfway to cracking up. I was all alone. And I had no idea that people went around kidnapping children or that he'd do the same thing with you.'

But as I listened to her giving evidence, flashing back to the moment I first saw her, it came crashing down upon me once again.

'Did you abduct Laetitia?' the judge asked the accused.

'It was Sabine's idea. She was driving me mad, begging me to get her a friend.'

I wanted the earth to swallow me up. Was I going to be faced with this all my life? Laetitia glanced at me, and gave me a little look, as if to say *Sorry* . . . We'd talked about it before she gave her evidence. I didn't want to rub salt into the wound, but the truth was that her coming had saved my life.

'And don't forget, I wasn't lucky enough to have had any

witnesses when he grabbed me. So, if you hadn't come . . . I'm sorry that it had to be you, but otherwise I would have been dead. Instead I am alive, and so are you. I know that I've screwed up your life, and I still get angry thinking about just how stupid I was, but if I hadn't – well. It's only because of you and the witnesses that we can even have this conversation.'

I will never be able to forgive myself, even though I know that Laetitia herself bears me no grudge. 'Listen,' she said to me shortly after she'd given evidence and I had said that I deserved to be in the glass box among the accused. 'If it hadn't been me, it would have been someone else. And you didn't set out to harm me. He did. He put me through all that hell, not you.'

Later, when I was being interviewed by the press, a journalist asked me if Laetitia and I were bosom buddies. 'Let's just say that we have things in common,' I replied. 'But we're not childhood friends, or school friends. Laetitia and I are sisters in sorrow.'

Dutroux's wife had tried the same thing with Laetitia that she had tried with me, but Laetitia didn't even let her finish the sentence.

'I don't want to hear how sorry you are. It's too late.'

Dutroux also attempted the same sick line: 'I would like to present my most humble apologies . . . I accept now that I hurt you . . .' It was exhausting. He'd have done better to just shut up. And anyway, it was all meaningless. This scumbag was incapable of guilt, let alone remorse. He didn't give a damn what he did to the children he kidnapped, letting them starve, burying them alive. This performance was just a different method of putting himself through 'his paces' in front of the court. He didn't fool me. In fact, I expected nothing less. He was playing true to type: vain, manipulative, underhand, incapable of telling the truth. As I left the court after Laetitia's turn in the witness box, I was asked by a television crew what I thought of his apology.

'I hope he chokes on it,' I said.

The press had said that I had beaten him through sheer strength of character, an example, they said, of what could be achieved with pluck and grit. Good. But I wouldn't be vindicated until I'd heard the verdict and sentence – and there was one final ordeal to overcome.

The court had decided that a guided tour of the sights would be appropriate. Judges, jurors, lawyers, witnesses – and the accused – were to see for themselves just what the hidy-hole was like.

Laetitia and I were, naturally, key figures in this little drama. On the journey to Marcinelle we began to giggle. 'I tell you, if I see a spider down there, I'm going to scream,' she whispered, 'so if I do, you mustn't worry.'

And I reminded her how every time we'd gone down the stairs to the cellar he'd say, 'No touching the walls, mind, or I'll give you what for.' I have no idea what it had been about this particular wall, as I made sure I touched every other wall in the place just to show him.

'Do you think the dinosaur poster will still be there?' Laetitia asked. I knew her memories were much vaguer than mine. She was also shocked, at times, by my black humour.

As soon as we arrived outside the house of horrors, which was screened off from the eyes of the curious by tarpaulins, it was a different story. We had to wait till everyone else – or nearly everyone else – went in front of us. The jurors, the judges, the victim-plaintiffs – one by one they filed past, went down, and re-emerged looking as white as sheets.

'Have you noticed their expressions?' Laetitia whispered. I had.

Laetitia went down before I did. Only when I saw her come back did I feel really frightened. If she had reacted like that – having been down there only six days – then the chances were I wouldn't be able to handle it at all. I felt as though every bit of blood had drained out of me. My mouth went dry and anxiety washed over me in waves.

Maître Rivière and Maître Parisse came with me. The front room was pretty much exactly as I had remembered it, I told them – a complete tip as it always was. But I felt okay.

Where next? I wondered. The Calvary room or the cellar?

I decided on the cellar. I went down the stairs without touching the wall, but this time simply because they'd put up a rope to make it easier for the old people. The stairway itself was quite narrow. There were twelve steps. Before, I used to count them every time I went back down. When it came to the rat-hole, I had to go in alone, since it was obviously far too small to take the three of us at one go.

My reaction was instantaneous. Suddenly I was back there again and, just like in a film, the scenes flashed across my inner eye, in jump-cut, freeze-frame: me doing my school work, writing my letters, feeling terrified during the power cut, and my frenzy of trying to get the light and the ventilator to work. A chalk circle had been drawn by the police around where Julie had written her name on the wall; to my shame, I had never noticed it when I was there. If I had, I wondered, would it have meant anything to me? At least I could have pointed it out to the police. The hell-hole was minuscule, even smaller and more horrible and suffocating than I had remembered.

Then it was back upstairs, to the room with the bunk beds. In the intervening years they had rusted, and the ladder had been sawn away. The dinosaur poster had disappeared. This room, too, seemed smaller.

Next door, in the Calvary room, everything was as it had been: the bed, the curtains, the table at the end of the bed with the jigsaw that drove me mad. It had already been started by the time I arrived. When I was allowed a bit of peace – when he was watching some crap on television – I would gaze up at the ceiling, or sometimes peer across at the jigsaw. Two or three times, I even tried to do it. By the end, it was nearly finished, only a few more pieces to go. But it was one of those countryside scenes, mostly bluey-grey or green, so it was more difficult than it looked. I'd never thought to ask who had started it. It could even be that all four of them had looked at it before me. I never finished it. One day, I was so irritated that I had given it a little shove. And I'd realised how I hated it, and the house, and how I had to get out, though I knew that I would never find a way . . .

I was still in the house when Laetitia came to find me, and we stood together as we had done eight years before. Someone said that I looked about twelve, but the reason I was pale was that I could hear that the bastard was about to take his turn around his former HQ, handcuffed and wearing a bullet-proof vest.

'I can't believe what a mess they've made of this place,' I heard him say as he came into the front room.

I looked at Laetitia, who had turned and was on her way out.

'I'm staying,' I whispered. 'I want to see if this time he will look me in the eye, now that there's no glass cage to hide behind.'

And I stepped out into his path, stopped, and looked straight at him. He only stared at the ground.

'Scumbag,' I said. Just the one word. The only one that came to me.

Someone took my arm and moved me to one side. The next thing I knew was Laetitia talking to me.

'Deep breath. Okay, now another one. Come on, let's get you out of here.' The place was surrounded by police vans, tarpaulins, barricades, so I just stood to one side. I don't know whether I was angry at myself for having broken down, or angry at him for having the right to be there at all. When I saw him come out of that charnel house, I was overwhelmed by another surge of anger. There was more I wanted to say. If necessary, I would just plant myself in front of the door to the van, refuse to move and simply force him to look at me. I'd had enough of this eyes-to-the-ground weaselling out.

But I'd been warned after the last time that I risked being in contempt of court, so I did nothing. I stayed where I was. I was strong. Even through my tears. I was uncowed, unbowed. I was not frightened of him. It wasn't he who had frightened me. It was just the house, the hole, the room that had caught me unawares.

I hadn't realised that among the listless queue of people to have visited the house, there had been journalists, and the next day, one word was spread across the front pages:

'Scumbag.'

That made me feel better. But I just wished I'd been able to say what I wanted to – either that afternoon, or the afternoon eight years before, the afternoon of 15 August 1996:

See what you've done? See where it's got you? Happy now, are you? Words that had come to me when I was twelve, words that had never gone away. Perhaps I should have argued that I should have done the house tour with him. So that he'd get it into his great thick psychopathic skull that it was over. Once and for all. 'You see? I'm not afraid any more. I've even come along here with you!'

But no. Even the stroppy little madam knew her limits.

In an emotional final speech to the jury, Maître Rivière told the court how I had managed to reinvent myself – first as a little girl, then as a young woman – to become the person I was now, testifying in front of this court and facing my abuser. 'There is something Mademoiselle Dardenne wants you to know,' he said, addressing his words to the glass box. 'When she was sixteen years of age, she fell in love. The idea of taking this love to its natural conclusion filled her with fear and humiliation. How could she explain that between her and her young man lay your foul breath, Dutroux, the stench of rancid meat and fetid feet? And yet, in spite of this, they made love. Yes, *made love*, Dutroux! A joy you have never experienced. And that is this brave young woman's revenge.'

When the speech was over, he had the nerve to murmur that he 'wasn't jealous' and that he wished me a happy life. It defies belief.

Now it was down to the court and the nine jurors. The public prosecutor's final speech was damning. No nonsense about a nationwide, big-wheel web, but a conspiracy of low-rent crooks, specialists in abduction, rape, incarceration, assassination and murder. To reach a final verdict the jurors had to answer two hundred and forty-three questions with either a Yes or a No.

The sentence would take no account of mitigating circumstances. There were none. Life imprisonment with no review for at least ten years for Dutroux: he would have to drink his bitter cup right to the end, just like his coffee. For his wife, Michèle Martin: thirty years. Lelièvre: twenty-five years. And five years for Nihoul, trafficker in prostitutes and thief but someone who, in the eyes of the jury, had nothing to do with 'the network', despite Dutroux's central claim. The theory of those first brave investigators, Michel Dumoulin and Lucien Masson, and that of the Investigating Judge Langlois had finally been vindicated: The 'man who looked after me' was a lone sexual deviant.

It was over. The accused had the right, of course, to lodge appeals with the High Court if they felt they had been unjustly treated. The lone sexual deviant has decided to do just that, so I can't sheathe my flaming sword quite yet. I have no means of entering the mind of a psychopath, lone or otherwise, but I would really like to understand what goes on in there, and why.

It might help to enlighten me.

After four months of madness, I picked up the reins of my life again, went back to my job, back to the commuter train, back to the sidelong glances. Once someone had the nerve to ask for my autograph, and I'm not sorry to say that he got a lot more than he expected. I was reminded again of what it had felt like, having to beat a path through the crowd of people and journalists in front of the court. And I decided I was not prepared to spend the rest of my life beating a path through a world of voyeurs.

So I decided to disappear once more – voluntarily this time – to try and fit together the dark pieces of this dark and sprawling puzzle, in the middle of which I somehow managed to survive. Then to tidy those pieces away in my own memory bank, but in a form which I hope will be once and for all and for ever: a book on a shelf.

And then to forget.

Sabine Dardenne
Summer 2004

ACKNOWLEDGEMENTS

Special thanks are due to

Marie-Thérèse Cuny and Philippe Robinet, and everyone involved in making this book happen;

Maître Rivière and Maître Parisse, whom I trust implicitly. They kept me going, advised me, protected me – and still do;

My grandmother, who is sadly no longer with us, and whom I miss dreadfully;

My mum, in spite of our differences: we only have one!
My father;

211

My partner, whom I decided to keep at arm's-length during the trial, but who has been a huge support and still is, together with his family;

Jacques Langlois, the Investigating Judge;

Michel Dumoulin, whom I hold in high esteem, and all the other investigators from the Neufchateau unit.

I would also like to thank

My big sister, for being there for me;

My friend Davina, who always has time for me;

Laetitia who, in spite of our previous differences, kept me going through the trial, and we are still in touch;

Le Château du Pont d'Oye, where we stayed for four months;

Commissioners Shull and Simon, who made sure that the mechanics of the trial went as smoothly as possible for me;

Jean-Marc and Anne Lefebvre, who always welcomed me with open arms;

Thierry Schamp, who spent the whole of 27 April 2004 waiting in his car, in case I had a problem during the visit to the house where I was held captive;

The staff of the restaurant Tante Laure, who fed us so valiantly;

Those journalists who supported me, and who treated me fairly;

My superiors at work, who gave me the time to attend the trial without pressure.

And I would like to thank the following people for a variety of
reasons. Their names are listed alphabetically:

André Colin
Jean-Marc Connerotte
Robert and Andrée Flavegèce
Jean Lambrecks
Jean-Denis Lejeune
Lucien Masson
Philippe Morandini
Bernard Richard
Investigating Judge Tollebeeck and the investigators based at
Tournai
Yves and Josianne Vandevyver

Penelope Dening would like to thank Nicolas Brooke for his
help in de-mystifying the Belgian judicial system.

I Know Why the Caged Bird Sings

By Maya Angelou

'Verve, nerve and joy in her own talents effervesce throughout this book' Julia O'Faolain

'Its humour, even in the face of appalling discrimination, is robust. Autobiographical writing at its very best' Philip Oakes

In this first volume of her extraordinary autobiography, Maya Angelou beautifully evokes her childhood in the American South of the 1930s. She and her brother live with their grandmother, in Stamps, Arkansas, where Maya learns the power of the 'whitefolks' at the other end of town. A visit to her adored mother ends in tragedy when Maya is raped by her mother's lover. But her extraordinary sense of wholeness emerges; she discovers the pleasures of dance and drama and gives birth to a treasured son.

Desert Flower

By Waris Dirie

'A story that traverses continents, spans the worlds of human experience and human pain . . . Waris Dirie was a victim once, but she never will be again. She is still fighting, still using her beauty and courage to take what she has learned to try and put things right' *Sunday Express*

'She was circumcised at five, fled an arranged marriage at 12, then became a Pirelli girl in her teens. Now, Waris Dirie is an ambassador for the UN' *Observer*

'Born a Somalian nomad, by the time she made it as a top model, she'd survived genital mutilation and a face-off with a tiger . . . She's now a UN special Ambassador. Take a cue from Waris's charm and courage' *Company*

'Her first job was for a Pirelli calendar shoot – with Terence Donovan – along with a young unknown girl from Streatham called Naomi Campbell . . . Now author of a book, published in 14 languages, which has had such a powerful effect on Elton John that he has bought the movie rights' *The Times*

**You can order other Virago titles through our website: *www.virago.co.uk*
or by using the order form below**

  I Know Why the Caged Bird Sings   Maya Angelou   £7.99
☐ Desert Flower   Waris Dirie   £7.99

*The prices shown above are correct at time of going to press. However, the
publishers reserve the right to increase prices on covers from those previously
advertised, without further notice.*

Virago

Please allow for postage and packing: **Free UK delivery.**
Europe: add 25% of retail price; Rest of World: 45% of retail price.

To order any of the above or any other Virago titles, please call our credit
card orderline or fill in this coupon and send/fax it to:

Virago, PO Box 121, Kettering, Northants NN14 4ZQ
Fax: 01832 733076   Tel: 01832 737526
Email: aspenhouse@FSBDial.co.uk

☐ I enclose a UK bank cheque made payable to Virago for £ . . . .
☐ Please charge £ . . . . . . to my Visa/Mastercard/Eurocard

Expiry Date | | | | | Switch Issue No. | | |

NAME (BLOCK LETTERS please) . . . .
ADDRESS . . . .

. . . .

. . . .

Postcode . . . . Telephone . . . .
Signature . . . .

Please allow 28 days for delivery within the UK. Offer subject to price and availability.
Please do not send any further mailings from companies carefully selected by Virago ☐